Perspectives from ERIC/EECE: A Monograph Series

Reflections on the
Reggio Emilia Approach

a collection of papers by

Lilian G. Katz
Brenda Fyfe
Rebecca New
George Forman
Carlina Rinaldi
Giordana Rabitti
Carolyn Edwards,
Lella Gandini,
and John Nimmo

edited by

Lilian G. Katz
Bernard Cesarone

December 1994

Catalog No. 215

Perspectives from ERIC/EECE: A Monograph Series, No. 6

ERIC Clearinghouse on Elementary
and Early Childhood Education
805 W. Pennsylvania
Urbana, IL 61801-4897

This publication was prepared with funding from the Office of
Educational Research and Improvement, U.S. Department of Education,
under contract no. DERR93002007.
The opinions expressed in this publication do not necessarily reflect
the positions or policies of OERI or the Department of Education.

Reprinted in Italy, June, 1995, with the permission of the
ERIC Clearinghouse on Elementary and Early Childhood Education
by Edizioni Junior srl, Via Pescaria, 32 - 24123 Bergamo (Italy)
Fax 0039/35/236322

Perspectives from ERIC/EECE:
A Monograph Series

In the course of carrying out its mission, the ERIC Clearinghouse on Elementary and Early Childhood Education (ERIC/EECE) annually abstracts and indexes thousands of documents and journal articles, responds to thousands of questions, and exchanges views with countless educators around the country at conferences and meetings. With this monograph we launch a new series of analyses and summaries addressed to topics frequently raised by ERIC/EECE users. Publications in this series will address current issues in all areas of the clearinghouse scope of interest: early, elementary, and middle level education; child development; child care; the child in the family; the family in society; and issues related to the dissemination of information. These publications are intended to suggest the consideration of new ways of looking at current issues. Suggestions of topics and authors for this series are always welcome. Please contact the clearinghouse with suggestions or comments:

ERIC/EECE University of Illinois
805 W. Pennsylvania
Urbana, IL 61801
Telephone: 217-333-1386
800 telephone: 800-583-4135
Fax: 217-333-3767
Email:ericeece@ux1.cso.uiuc.edu

Preface

Early childhood educators around the world continue to be deeply inspired and enlightened by what we are learning from the preprimary schools of Reggio Emilia. We are pleased to present this collection of recent papers representing a variety of perspectives on the implications of the Reggio Emilia approach to early education.

Four of the papers were presented at the Study Seminar on the Experience of the Municipal Infant-Toddler Centers and Preprimary Schools of Reggio Emilia, Italy (June 1994). My paper takes up a series of issues-related problems that warrant consideration when attempting to adapt and adopt the Reggio Emilia approach in the United States. Brenda Fyfe shares important insights gained by a group of teachers in the St. Louis area as they face the daily practical problems involved in implementing the approach in their own classrooms. Rebecca New places the issues in the larger cultural context in which early childhood practitioners work and draws our attention to the similarities and differences in which teachers in Italy and the United States perform their daily work and how they influence their efforts. George Forman focuses on the important role of graphic 'languages' in young children's learning and deepens our understanding of the potential value of drawing in young children's learning.

Carlina Rinaldi, pedagogista of the municipal preprimary schools of Reggio Emilia, outlines their unique approach to staff development and staff relationships, one of the central components of their approach. Giordana Rabbitti's paper is based on her detailed case study of a project conducted in one of the preprimary schools in Reggio Emilia that gives us the flavor of the day-to-day implementation of their approach.

The paper by Edwards, Gandini and Nimmo focuses on how teachers in three communities, two in Italy and one in the United States, define their roles and their beliefs about the nature of children as learners. While the seven papers included in this collection were prompted by different purposes and occasions, they offer a rich mixture of ideas and information about early childhood education at its best. We are grateful to the authors for their willingness to share their insights and experience.

Lilian G. Katz
November 1994

Images from the World:
Study Seminar on the Experience
of the Municipal Infant-Toddler Centers
and Preprimary Schools of Reggio Emilia, Italy

Lilian G. Katz, Ph.D
University of Illinois - Urbana, Illinois

Editor's Note: This paper was the opening address presented at the Study Seminar on the Experience of the Municipal Infant-Toddler Centers and Preprimary Schools of Reggio Emilia on June 6, 1994, in Reggio Emilia, Italy.

The title of this presentation "Images from the World" was given to me by Loris Malaguzzi in a letter, dated January 24th, 1994, written very shortly before his untimely death. I quote from his letter:
I ask you to open the seminar with a report that recalls and widens the reflection on our experience and that explains the nature, the reasons, and the goals of this approach and these interests. A report that should include a comparison able to furnish a better knowledge of the policies and the educational theories that you have learned during your trips and international travels. Your report should give to the seminar the lines of an open discussion, of new interrogatives, of new hypotheses with reference to the social, cultural, and scientific changes. I know that I ask you a lot. But I admit that we also need to have wider visions, and the seminar will offer us an occasion of great privilege.

In the notes I have from a message he also sent through Lella Gandini, I know that he had indicated a desire to have an overview of "the latest tendencies, issues, and trends in the field, around the world, and certainly in the U.S.A." Through Lella he also relayed the hope that this seminar would be a "re- reading of the experience of Reggio Emilia, and discussion about the resources needed to go on with what is being learned here." He is very deeply missed today.

During my visit here to Reggio Emilia two weeks ago, I had the opportunity to discuss this assignment in more detail with Carlina Rinaldi. She expressed the wish that this seminar would be about more than the Reggio approach as we now call it and that it would also be a context for exchange and reflection, for the development of our knowledge and theory, for agreement and disagreement, for discoveries of our differences. She indicated the hope that we would continue to challenge and be challenged, to create a community, and to provide an opportunity to learn and to support each other as we move ahead, in particular how we move ahead in helping others through our training efforts to benefit from what is being learned here. She also expressed the hope that we would continue to provide an opportunity to learn how Reggio Children, a foundation whose purpose is to increase awareness of the Reggio Emilia approach to the education of young children, can continue to help those of us who are interested in the Reggio Emilia approach, That having been said, it has been difficult to choose what to present especially in view of the fact that so many of you here know much more about the Reggio Emilia approach than I do and are already actively involved in training and implementing it yourselves. Our friends here from Scandinavia have even longer experience than we in the United States in implementing the Reggio Emilia approach. I hope we can learn from their experience also.

I decided to begin with a few observations of the "world scene," then take up some problems involved in thinking about where we might go from here, and finally to offer a few concluding points. All in all, you will not be surprised that I have not found anything to say that has not already been said and that you don't already know!

I. World View

My international experience began exactly twenty years ago with a mission for UNESCO to offer training in preschool methods on one of the Caribbean islands, helping teachers working under difficult structural conditions (space, numbers of children, etc.), but in a very favorable cultural environment marked by a deep and longstanding commitment to the education of all of the island's children.

During this twenty-year period, I have visited and worked with preprimary educators on every continent many times over. I have seen some inspiring practices over the years in many places, such as New Zealand, the U.K. during the so-called Plowden years, Northern Germany, and places scattered around our own country. I have also seen very sad examples, such as child development centers all over India struggling with extremely difficult conditions, a child care facility in a steel factory in China serving 800 very young children in very crowded conditions, and examples across our own country as well.

But never had I seen before any provisions for young children as good as those I have seen during my six previous visits to Reggio Emilia and I have been in eight of the schools, including two infant-toddler centers. There is no need to rehearse here the basis of that statement. You all know it well from your own observations and visits. The main point is that in Reggio Emilia we see clearer evidence than in all our own collected works to suggest that we have been right all along:

• All young children have active and lively minds from the start.
• The basic dispositions to make sense of experience, investigate it, care about others, relate to them, and adapt to their physical and cultural environment are dispositions within children from the start.
• These in-born dispositions can flourish deepen and strengthen under the right conditions.

From our colleagues here in Reggio Emilia, we are learning a great deal about those conditions. This is not an appropriate moment to spell out those conditions, but I trust we will discuss them in detail as the week proceeds. I must add, furthermore, that a close look at the Reggio approach shows how to transform into reality one of the major cliches of our field the importance of addressing "the whole child."

To continue with the world perspective, I have been involved in the IEA (International Association for Educational Evaluation, based in Enschede, The Netherlands) study of preprimary education in fourteen countries since its inception in 1981. The data, about to be published (Olmsted & Weikart, in press), include an investigation of the level of parental satisfaction in ten of these countries (Belgium, China, Finland, Germany, Hong Kong, Nigeria, Portugal, Spain, Thailand, and the United States) with the preprimary provisions for their children. With one exception, in all countries nearly 100 percent of the parents reported being satisfied with their services. Hong Kong was the exception because a small proportion of parents were dissatisfied, either because the programs were too academic or not sufficiently so.

Yet in none of these countries were the early childhood experts satisfied with these programs. How can these findings be interpreted? There are at least two possibilities that come to mind:

• First, parents and experts differ because the latter are more keenly aware of the range of possible program features or potentialities than parents are. Early childhood specialists like most of us here, at least speaking for myself see the typical quality of preprimary programs as *missed opportunities* to significantly enhance young children's physical, social, and intellectual development. In the United States indeed, I see the *typical* quality of preschool and primary education as a serious waste of children's minds.

• Second, if parents feel truly dissatisfied with their preprimary programs, yet must place their children in them, they would surely have to feel some guilt. I will return to this theme later.

Kagitcibasi of Turkey, an international authority on these issues, as cited in Olmsted (1994), said of these data that

in every country much work is needed to educate parents, to raise their expectations concerning services for children, to encourage them to demand better services, and in general, to create public awareness of the importance of early child care and education. (p. 10)

In the case of the United States at least, I am fairly convinced that little will happen to improve the typical quality of early childhood provisions especially in child care programs until parents demand it and demand support for staff salaries in particular. But this expectation raises two further issues. First, parents of young children are, by definition, a "transient" population. Their children are preschoolers for a very short time, even though it often seems very long to them! However, by the time the parents of preschoolers become aware of how much program improvement is needed, their children move on to the elementary school, and their parents' concerns shift with them.

Second, particularly in child care, if we urge parents to demand better quality, we may exacerbate their sense of guilt about placing their children in poor quality environments, and in our country, mothers who work already feel guilty about giving their young children into the care of others for most of their waking hours. So, what does this imply about next steps? I will return to this issue later.

The only other comment I can make about the world view at this point is that during the last several decades, with the help of many educators, developmental psychologists, and researchers, we have succeeded in convincing even the policymakers around the world that the early years are sufficiently important to warrant their attention.

In other words, we have succeeded in spreading the idea of the "primacy effect" namely, that the earliest events in life are the most important and formative ones and are the critical determinants of the long course of development. According to Michael Lewis (1994), an American psychologist, we may in fact have overstated the "primacy effect," suggesting that we must worry about appropriate education and experience throughout development. For example, it may be that early neglect and early damage cannot be reversed later on. However, it does not necessarily follow that early well-being and healthy functioning cannot be extinguished when it becomes maladaptive in the context of traditional schooling and oppressive social conditions. Human adaptability may be our greatest strength as well as our greatest weakness. In fact, Diana Slaughter-DeFoe (1994), reporting on a longitudinal study of children in the Chicago area, shows that the children who thrived best in the company of good preschool teachers were the ones who subsequently dropped out of school earlier and more often than others because they found their schools *uninteresting*, if not boring.

Nevertheless, I am aware of a clear trend in the United States in preprimary and primary schools of increasing interest in developmentally appropriate practices, even though we know this concept is in need of further refinement (this process of refinement is now under way). Similarly, the current widespread and increasing interest in Howard Gardner's ideas, in the project approach, in "whole language" teaching, in "situated learning" *(der Situationsansatz)*,[1] in the "integrated curriculum," and in the Reggio Emilia approach are also clear, current trends in the United States. And it is the latter that brings us all together here today. So I would like to turn our attention to the problems confronting us as we consider next steps in applying what we are learning from our friends here.

II. What Should We Think about for Next Steps?

One of the main goals of this seminar is to share our ideas about how to help our colleagues at home to learn from the Reggio experience. I want to take up some of the issues involved in this effort, first by looking briefly at the terminology we use in discussions of change. Second, I will address some concerns about the adaptation of innovations in general. And third, I will pose some questions about issues in adapting the Reggio Emilia approach in particular.

Terminology

On occasions like this, it seems useful to explore the topic by looking closely at the terms we might use. Here are some that are often employed in discussions of change in practices.

[1] See especially J. Zimmer (1994).

1. **Adaptation**. What do we mean when we speak of adapting an innovation, approach, or other new practices? According to my dictionary, to adapt is to make something suitable to some requirements or more suitable to new requirements; to adjust or to modify fittingly.

2. **Adoption**. This term is often used in discourse about changes in practices. The dictionary suggests that it means to choose, to take to oneself, to make one's own by selection or assent; to make as one's own as in adopting a child or to vote to adopt a resolution or motion.

3. **Translation**. (This term was suggested by Carlina Rinaldi and perhaps has a particular meaning in Italian speaking of translation!) The most common meaning is to turn something written or spoken from one language into another; to change something into another form; to bear, carry, or remove from one place to another. (Incidentally, my dictionary points out that in religious discourse, translation also means "to convey or remove to heaven without death." This is not without relevance to our deliberations here!)

4. **Implementation**. As a noun, the term *implement* refers to an instrument, as in farm implements or tools. As a verb it means "to execute as a piece of work." However, the Latin root *implere* means to fill up.

5. **Transformation**. This term means to change form, to change to something of a different form, or to change in appearance, nature, or character, *but without loss of value*, as in the use of an electrical transformer.

These terms indicate various kinds of change. Which of these terms best corresponds to what each of us hopes to do, or should try to do?

Issues in Adaptation in General

Doyle and Ponder (1977-78) put forward an interesting analysis of some of these issues under the heading "The Practicality Ethic in Teacher Decision-Making." According to their analysis, the practicality ethic has three components. When teachers are faced with pressure to adopt (Doyle and Ponder's term) an innovation, they make their decision on the basis of three criteria, paraphrased here in the form of questions teachers might ask of themselves or others:

1. **Congruence**. Is the innovation congruent with my current practices? Does it advance or strengthen what I am now doing? I might add here that a teacher might also ask: Does this innovation suggest that what I have been doing up to now was all wrong?! (Sue Bredekamp [1993] alluded to this reaction in her sensitive account of her first visit to Reggio Emilia.)

2. **Resources**. Will those who urge me to change provide me with the necessary resources (e.g., time, space, materials, staff) to make implementation possible, feasible, and practical?

3. **Cost-Reward Relationship**. Given the cost in terms of time and energy required to adopt the proposed innovation, will it provide me with sufficient rewards to make it worthwhile? In particular, will the "psychic" rewards be great enough in terms of children's interest, enthusiasm, and cooperation; parents' approval and appreciation; and administrators' approval? The amount of effort is deemed acceptable if the teacher is reasonably certain that the responses of the children and relevant others to the new practices will be positive, if not enthusiastic.

Doyle and Ponder suggest that, when the answers to these questions are largely negative, teachers discard the proposed innovation as "impractical." I suggest that we all might consider these three criteria of the practicality ethic before rushing into conversion, adaptation, adoption, incorporation, and implementation of a change in practices.

Adaptation of the Reggio Emilia Approach in Particular

As we think about adaptation of the Reggio Emilia approach in particular, here are some questions that come to mind:
1. Is the Reggio Emilia approach adaptable? Can it be made suitable to our context? Can it be adjusted to fit our situations, cultures, and conditions? What might be some of the main obstacles?
2. There are many elements that contribute to the Reggio Emilia approach. Our friends here in Reggio Emilia frequently point out that all of the elements of their approach must be in place to make it work. This makes the task of adoption so daunting that it may lead to discouragement at the outset. All the elements that constitute the Reggio Emilia approach took many years to develop. Which elements of the approach are most or least adaptable in each of our own contexts? How many years would we need to get to this point in the United States?

• **Physical features**. The arrangements and kinds of space available in the schools seem a central element of the schools' work. How many of the features of this element can we realistically expect to adopt? How long would it take?

• **Parental involvement**. This is a serious concern we all have shared for a long time. Can we emulate the success of Reggio Emilia along these lines? How long would it take? How should we begin?

Sometimes I wonder if Reggio Emilia's outstanding success with parental involvement is due to the extraordinary quality of the children's experiences, rather than the reverse. In other words, my hypothesis (I emphasize that this is a hypothesis and Loris wanted hypotheses) is that parents become involved, in large part, because of the quality of the experiences of their children, and that this quality is not simply the consequence or result of high parental involvement.[2]
If this is so, then we might try working directly and wholeheartedly at improving the quality of the children's in-school experiences as a way to draw parents' support and loyalty, rather than try to adapt or adopt the Reggio Emilia approach as a consequence of parental support. Perhaps

Amelia Gambetti, Ann Lewin, Brenda Fyfe, and others here who are already trying to implement the Reggio Emilia approach in the U.S. can tell us their reactions to this hypothesis.

It has been my experience in working with teachers implementing the project approach (Katz & Chard, 1989) that children's enthusiasm and eagerness to come to school to work on the projects have impressed their parents more than any other parental involvement strategy used. Perhaps there is a dynamic phenomenon in this matter such that good work with children brings in the parents, and their involvement leads teachers to strengthen their work with children. In other words, I am hypothesizing a kind of cyclic phenomenon such that good in-classroom practices engage or capture the parents' interest and provide a context for their involvement, and that these parental responses encourage teachers' continued experimentation, growth, and learning, which further invite and entice the parents' involvement, which in turn supports teachers' commitment, and so forth, in a positive cycle.

• **Collaboration**. We have all been impressed with Reggio Emilia's commitment to collaborative relationships among all the adults involved in their work. I am told that in this part of Italy there is a longstanding tradition of cooperatives and joint efforts that we in the United States generally do not share. How can we hope to or begin to emulate or adopt such a style of work?

• **Documentation**. The contribution of documentation to the work of our Reggio colleagues is also convincing and very impressive. How much staff time and energy does good documentation require? What other kinds of resources are required to yield such a high quality of documentation? How adaptable is this central feature for each of us? How much documentation is enough?

• **Atelieristi**. How many of us can hope to incorporate an atelierista, or a teacher trained in art education, into our programs? How much of the Reggio Emilia approach can be adapted without the constant presence of a skilled atelierista? Or, for that matter, how important to the whole effort is the availability of an atelier, or art workshop?

• **Pedagogisti**. The pedagogical and other kinds of leadership provided by the pedagogista seem to me to be a *sine qua non*. Indeed, the development of the pedagogical practices in Reggio Emilia seems to be almost entirely dependent on the in-service or staff development component of their approach. But not all in-service or staff development is the same! What seems to characterize the Reggio Emilia

---

[2] It seems to me that a large proportion of young children's activities in U.S. schools are unlikely to engage the interest, participation, enthusiasm, or loyalty of their parents, compared with the way the kind of work of the Reggio Emilia Children can enlist parents' interest and support. I have in mind here the identical and unimaginative snowflakes and Valentine's cards made by whole classes of Kindergarten children that I saw this winter. How could parents be drawn into discussing such children's work with their teachers?

approach is the constant availability of the pedagogisti, a sufficient number of them to make it possible for them to know every teacher well, and indeed, to know every family. How much of such support do we need and can we expect for such services?

• **Three-year group**. One of the features of the Reggio Emilia approach that seems to provide a variety of benefits is that children stay with the same teachers during their three years in the schools. How implementable is such a practice in our preschools and primary schools? I would hope that it might be partially accomplished through mixed-age grouping. Interest in mixed-age grouping continues to grow, and a number of school systems in the United State are implementing that practice already. We might hear more about this from our friends here from Kentucky, where the whole state is now requiring mixed-age grouping from kindergarten through third grade.

• **Project work**. Involving young children in project work namely, extended, in-depth studies of significant topics is not unique to Reggio Emilia. It was introduced in the United States earlier in this century,[3] and was done exquisitely in Britain during the so-called Plowden years (1960s and 1970s). As far as I know, the Reggio Emilia schools have taken this pedagogical practice further than anyone else.[4] In particular, they have succeeded in making the "graphic languages" a major aspect of young children's project work in fresh new ways. [5]

III. Concluding Comments

There is of course much more that could be said about all of this. I want to conclude with a few points on bringing about change. Many of you are already familiar with the work of Michael Fullan (see Fullan and Miles, 1992) of Canada and his insights into the complexities of bringing about *lasting* change. Temporary change is relatively easy. In the time we have today, it is not possible to do justice to all of Fullan's ideas. However, I want to emphasize that they are truly worthy of our attention in terms of the purposes of this seminar.

---

[3] A colleague recently sent me a book on the project method titled *Practical Problem Projects* by F. W. Rawcliffe, published in 1924 (see reference list)! Rawcliffe's words of seventy years ago seem very familiar: In the school where the project method is used, "almost all the traditional formality is gone. Discipline depends upon the public opinion of the class. Children engaged in project activities are too busy and happy to think of disorder. The old-time recitation is passing....In place of it, the teacher and children as a group are engaged in activities that are purposeful and pleasurable. The schoolroom has become a laboratory....Discussion, research, expression by means of reports, dialogs, debates, plays, drawing, construction, written composition these are the principal activities. Research is finding out, " and so forth.

[4] Some excellent project work was described by Susan Isaacs in the 1930s and 1940s. However, she worked primarily with relatively privileged children. See especially Isaacs (1930).

[5] Excellent work along these lines was also reported by Elwyn S. Richardson in New Zealand in the mid 1960s and early 1970s. See especially Elwyn S. Richardson (1972).

First of all, Fullan says that lasting change cannot be mandated from above. In fact, he says, mandates from above frequently make matters worse: "You can't mandate important changes, because they require skill, motivation, commitment, and discretionary judgment on the part of those who must change." He points out that goals in the absence of a theory are mere wishful thinking, especially in the absence of a theory of the change process. He also points out that there are many levels of change and that the complexities are staggering. He suggests that there are macro-level changes, such as in funding and policy matters. There are meso-level changes, perhaps in terms of staff deployment and practices such as age grouping. And there are micro-level changes, such as the nature of the intimate daily teacher-child interactions. Fullan calls for changes in school cultures, teacher-student relationships, values and expectations of the system, and so forth.

Of special interest to our deliberations here, I think, is Fullan's warning about the temptations to confuse changes in symbols with changes in substance. "Many of the political and policy-making bodies are concerned with symbols they want to appear to be doing something bold and new. Often, appearances are enough for political success!" (Fullan & Miles, 1992). I quote again:

Political time lines are at variance with the time lines for education reform. This difference often results in vague goals, unrealistic schedules, a preoccupation with symbols of reform (new legislation, task forces, commissions, and the like). (p. 746)

While symbols have a role, they can attract support and mobilize groups for action change in substance requires a lot of hard and clever work "on the ground." (p. 747)

"While we cannot have effective reform (change) without symbols, we can easily have symbols without effective reform... lack of real substance can lead to skepticism about all reforms and efforts toward change. (p. 747)

Another tendency Fullan mentions, to which the United States is especially vulnerable, is "fadism," part of a general temptation to look for the "quick fix," to go along with the latest trends, to react uncritically to endorsed innovations as they come and go. We here must be especially studious about explicating to our colleagues at home the complexity of the Reggio Emilia approach.

Fullan offers seven propositions to keep in mind for successful change:

1. **Change is learning-loaded with uncertainty.** He reminds us that anxiety, difficulties, and uncertainty are intrinsic to all successful change. All change involves learning, and all learning involves coming to understand and to be good at something new.

2. **Change is a journey, not a blueprint**. Fullan's message is not the traditional "plan, then do" but "do, then plan, and do, and plan some more, and do some more, and so forth." We can see these processes beautifully exemplified here in Reggio Emilia.

3. **Problems are our friends**. Improvement is a problem-rich process. Change threatens existing interests and routines, heightens uncertainty, and increases complexity. We cannot develop effective responses to complex situations unless we actively seek and confront real problems that are difficult to solve. In this sense, effective organizations "embrace problems," rather than avoid them.

4. **Change is resource-hungry**. Time is the salient issue, and time is an important, indispensable, and energy-demanding resource.

5. **Change requires the power to manage it**. For this, Fullan recommends openness and interaction among all those concerned with what is being changed. Openness means that we must all learn a lot about how to respond to complaints, frustrations, disagreements, and conflicts and see them as part of development.

6. **Change is systemic**. Here Fullan would agree with our Reggio friends that all parts of the system must be involved in the change simultaneously. He says that change must focus not just on structure, policy, and regulations, but on deeper issues of the culture of the system.

7. **All large-scale change is implemented locally**. Change cannot be accomplished from afar, but must involve those very people who will implement the new practices on a day-to-day level as well as the larger and more distant agencies involved.

I also want to urge all of you to reread Meg Barden's (1993) chapter in *The Hundred Languages of Children*. She reminds us that many of the ideas we are seeing in practice in Reggio Emilia have been practiced before, only to disappear from the scene in the face of a variety of difficulties often of a political nature but sometimes because those involved begin to quarrel among themselves.

So where are we now? As participants and members of the Reggio Children/U.S.A. group, what should we be thinking about now? What should or can each of us do now?

Fullan seems to agree with our friends in Reggio Emilia that all the elements of the approach must be addressed together. This is a tall order. If we can't do it all, should we do nothing at all? And if we decide that even though we can't do it all at once, we want to move ahead, where should we start? Should we and can we start at different places? For example, should some of us start with in-service training? Some with ateliers? Some with long-term projects? Some with documentation? But, of course, there has to be something worthwhile to document!

One thought that continues to haunt me is that perhaps we should be especially careful not to call our efforts "The Reggio Emilia approach," even if our work and our strategies are inspired by Reggio Emilia and are based on what we are learning from Reggio. There are several reasons behind this "specter." One is the obvious fact that it would take any of us a very long time to be worthy of that name.

Another is that *if we implement the Reggio Emilia approach insufficiently or inadequately we might unwittingly and inadvertently give it a bad name, cast doubts about it, and give the impression that it is just a passing fad.*

If we don't call our efforts the Reggio Emilia approach even though we are trying to implement, adopt, and adapt what we are learning from Reggio Emilia what should we call it? Why not call it developmentally appropriate practices? Surely the Reggio approach best exemplifies developmentally appropriate practices.

Another idea comes from what we know about what is called "perturbation theory." The easiest way to explain my thought here is to take a simple example of a perturbation. Imagine, if you will, a woman cycling at a good clip along a road without difficulty. Suddenly the front wheel collides with a small pebble in the road and is thrown off course. The rider falls, is seriously injured, and strikes up a very important relationship with a solicitous and helpful passerby, and her whole life changes fundamentally and forever. Perturbation theory suggests that *even very small items can have huge and lasting consequences.*

What we are really asking in our deliberations together to take what we are learning from our colleagues here to our own country, our own schools, and our own students is for huge and lasting consequences. My question is: *Is there a relatively small pebble we can put in place now that will ultimately have the large and lasting consequences we hope for?*

As I indicated at the beginning of this presentation, Loris Malaguzzi asked for hypotheses. As I suggested earlier, one of mine is that, if we focus our collective and individual energies *on the quality of the day-to-day interactions of children and their teachers* in their moments together so that they become as rich, interesting, engaging, satisfying, and meaningful as we can see here in the preprimary schools of Reggio Emilia, we will be shaping a pebble that could have very large consequences:

• It might attract the interest, involvement, and loyalty of parents better than all the incantations about parental involvement exclaimed in commission reports and similar dissemination materials.

• It would address children where they are now.

• We would all be learning about learning and about children's rich and lively minds and their amazing capacities to imagine, hypothesize, investigate, interact, and co-construct fresh understandings of their worlds.

• Our actions would speak more clearly and loudly than what we say.

• *And we would be doing what is right addressing the day-to-day quality of children's lives.*

That is not to say that we should not also be working at the other important elements we have been learning about. But we have to start somewhere, and our children cannot wait until all the elements are in place.

I suggest also that we should take a developmental approach to ourselves and the teachers to whom we are responsible (Katz, in press-a). We must also be sensitive to where their zones of proximal development (ZPD) are. Note that even though most of us use

Vygotsky's ZPD construct, he did not co-construct it with us. However, once we were exposed to the construct, it helped us to "learn" what we already knew, perhaps intuitively. The ZPD construct helps us to make sense of our own experience and, in my view, one of the main priorities of our work with young children is to help them make better, deeper, and more accurate sense of their own experience (Katz, in press-b). I believe our work with our students can be approached in a very similar way.

Furthermore, if it is true that one of the important responsibilities of a teacher is to "educate the attention" of children (Prawat, 1993), then perhaps we can start by "educating the attention" of our colleagues, teachers, and students, just as our friends in Reggio Emilia have so carefully been educating ours.

Finally, let us keep in mind the concerns of our colleagues here. As Carlina Rinaldi put it to me, in her usual thoughtful way: her concern is that "we see the Reggio Emilia experience and practices together as a treasure that we have in common, and we must be careful to look at it with love, respect, and care."

We are all deeply indebted to our colleagues in Reggio Emilia for showing us again and again what is possible when a whole community is deeply committed to its children. They are such a powerful, "strong" as they say inspiration to all of us. They help us to keep at it and not to give up. Their work is a challenge to the whole field around the whole world the challenge to provide early childhood education that is worthy of all our children.

References

BARDEN, M. (1993). A backward look: From Reggio Emilia to progressive education. In C. Edwards, L. Gandini, and G. Forman (Eds.), *The hundred languages of children: The Reggio Emilia approach to early childhood education* (pp. 283-295). Norwood, NJ: Ablex Publishing Corporation. ED 355 034.

BREDEKAMP, S. (1993). Reflections on Reggio Emilia. *Young Children* 49(1, November):13-15. EJ 474 756.

DOYLE, W., and G. PONDER. (1977-78). The practicality ethic in teacher decision-making. *Interchange* 8(3):1-12.

FULLAN, M.G., and M.B. MILES. (1992). Getting reform right: *What works* and what doesn't. *Phi Delta Kappan* 73(10, June):745-752. EJ 445 727.

ISAACS, S. (1930). *Intellectual growth in young children.* London: George Routledge & Sons, Ltd.

KATZ, L.G. (In press-a). Helping others with their teaching. In L.G. Katz (Ed.), *Talks with teachers of young children: A collection.* Norwood, NJ: Ablex Publishing Co. (For an earlier version of this paper, see ED 363 453.)

KATZ, L.G. (In press-b). Pedagogical issues in early childhood education. In L.G. Katz (Ed.), *Talks with teachers of young children: A collection.* Norwood, NJ: Ablex Publishing Co. (For an earlier version of this paper, see ED 321 840.)

KATZ, L.G., and S.C. CHARD. (1989). *Engaging children's minds: The project approach.* Norwood, NJ: Ablex Publishing Co.

LEWIS, M. (1994). *Development, history, and other problems of change.* Paper presented at the symposium on Advances in Early Childhood Education and Care, in honor of E. Kuno Beller, Free University of Berlin, May.

OLMSTED, P.P. (1994). Taking a global view: A 15-nation study. *High/Scope ReSource* 13(3):1, 9-12.

OLMSTED, P., and D. WEIKART. (Eds.). (In press). *Families speak: Early childhood care and education in 11 countries.* Ypsilanti, MI: High/Scope Foundation.

PRAWAT, R.S. (1993). The value of ideas: Problems versus possibilities in learning. *Educational Researcher* 22(6, August-September):5-16. EJ 471 979.

RAWCLIFFE, F.W. (1924). *Practical problem projects.* Chicago: R.E. Compton & Company.

RICHARDSON, E.S. (1972). *In the early world.* Wellington, New Zealand: New Zealand Council for Educational Research.

SLAUGHTER-DEFOE, D. (1994). *Teachers as leaders.* Paper presented at the Third Annual Conference of the National Association for the Education of Young Children's National Institute for Early Childhood Professional Development, Chicago, IL, June 4.

ZIMMER, J. (1994). *Experiences with the situational approach in Asia.* Paper presented at the symposium on Advances in Early Childhood Education and Care, in honor of E. Kuno Beller, Free University of Berlin, May.

Images from the United States: Using Ideas from the Reggio Emilia Experience with American Educators

Brenda Fyfe
Webster University - St. Louis, Missouri

Editor's Note: The author wishes to thank Louise Cadwell of the Reggio Emilia Grant Project in St. Louis, Missouri, and Jan Phillips of The College School in Webster Groves, Missouri, for their contributions in analyzing and synthesizing the content of this paper.

In the fall of 1991, *The Hundred Languages of Children* exhibit was brought to St. Louis, Missouri. It created tremendous interest in the detail and creativity of work by three-, four-, and five-year-olds from the schools of Reggio Emilia, Italy. A series of workshops by Lella Gandini, Baji Rankin, Pam Houk, Lilian Katz, Rebecca New, and Carolyn Edwards whetted the appetites of hundreds of St. Louis teachers. Over the next two years, more than fifty of these teachers went to Reggio Emilia to observe firsthand the program that produced such incredible depth of learning by preschool children.

In the summer of 1992, plans were made to begin a project to provide a system of professional development for teachers who wished to continue their study and implementation of the principles and practices of Reggio Emilia. A grant obtained from the Danforth Foundation made it possible to begin the project in the fall of 1992.

This paper describes the professional development system and some of the experiences and insights of teachers who have participated in it for the past two years.

Although the fifty educators involved have common interests and experiences in regard to the study of the Reggio Emilia approach, they have come into the project with different backgrounds of experience, levels of education, and understandings of constructivism, and from different kinds of work contexts. The project includes teachers of infants, toddlers, preschool-age children, kindergartners, and first and second graders. Art educators and administrators are also included. These educators work in private and public programs, including Head Start and public school districts, in both city and county locations. The families of the children served range from low to high socioeconomic status. Children with special needs are integrated into some of the schools.

The Professional Development System

The graphic in Figure 1 depicts the components of a professional development support system that has evolved over the first two years of our Danforth Foundation grant. When planning our project, we reviewed the literature on critical attributes of effective teacher development programs and ways to support change in schools (Costa, Garmston, & Lambert, 1988; Eisner, 1992; Fullan, 1990; Fullan & Stiegelbauer, 1991; Fullan & Miles, 1992; Hord et al., 1987); we studied the system of support for professional development established for teachers in Reggio Emilia; and we assessed the needs and interests of teachers, administrators, and parents in our project. We have attempted to establish a network of relations among all of the members of our learning community.

When devising professional development opportunities, we tried to keep in mind that "effective change facilitators work with people in an adaptive and systemic way, designing interventions for clients' needs, realizing that those needs exist in particular contexts and settings" (Hord et al., 1987, p. 7). Different responses and interventions are required for different people. Our system of support continues to grow and transform as we respond to needs and interests of the participants in the project. We keep abreast of these through discussions at group meetings, questionnaires, on-site consultation visits, and written professional development plans.

Individual or group professional development plans of teachers help bring focus to their study. Teachers have been strongly encouraged to collaborate, when possible, on group or partner professional development plans. Those who have chosen to do so have, as expected, had more incentive and opportunity to engage in discussion, reflection, and interpretation of their collective work.

These teachers may work toward common goals in the same ways (for example, by forming a study group to discuss shared readings). Or they may choose to work in different ways to reach a common goal and then come together to share experiences, reflections, and perspectives.

Even when teachers do not develop group or interdependent professional development plans, their written plans serve as vehicles for communication with other teachers and administrators.

Fig. 1 Professional Development System

Our format for professional development plans (see appendix) is derived from the work of Vartuli and Fyfe (1993). It asks teachers to (1) select goals, (2) identify methods of support that could help them achieve their goals, (3) plan a portfolio of evidence or data that could be collected through the year to help analyze progress toward goals, and (4) identify resources or additional information needed. In addition to helping teachers focus and plan for professional development, these written documents inform the project's co-directors of appropriate ways to allocate resources of the grant and plan for group learning opportunities. For example, in the second year of the project, forty percent of our teachers identified goals related to "learning better ways to work with parents as partners in the development, analysis, and implementation of curriculum." When Amelia Gambetti, George Forman, and Lella Gandini were invited to come to St. Louis to consult with us that year, we asked them to address this topic in their presentations.

Considerations and Interpretations of Change

Teachers in our project have made significant progress in their study and implementation of principles and practices from Reggio Emilia. A review of data collected from teacher journals, minutes of peer support group meetings, yearly evaluation questionnaires, interviews, and field notes from on-site consultation visits has begun to reveal some significant insights and changes in teaching practice. The next sections will present some of these and will focus on what appear to be some of the underlying barriers to change that are embedded in fundamental beliefs and values in our society. It will also present some teacher quandaries related to interpretations or misinterpretations of principles of developmentally appropriate practice.

Environmental Change

Many teachers choose to begin with environmental changes. They attempt to organize more aesthetically pleasing environments, to offer a richer and more varied assortment of materials, and to establish more physical connections with home. These are concrete ways in which teachers have embraced what they have seen as valuable features of the learning environments of the Reggio schools. Examples of such change at The College School, our demonstration site, include the following:
• The use of white paint, mirrors, natural light, and information panels to transform a dark and dreary entry into one that welcomes, invites, and communicates the joy of learning and a sense of belonging;
• The addition of an *atelier* to provide space for focused project work and development of the hundred languages;
• The addition of shelving with a new variety of found and purchased materials that can be used by children and teachers to explore and express ideas and feelings;
• The addition of household furniture such as a couch, chests, a wardrobe, chairs, lamps, and plants to develop a more homelike atmosphere;

• The addition of light tables to enable children to explore color and texture of materials with the added perspective of light;
• The cleaning, painting, and reorganizing of space to present orderly, uncluttered, comfortable, defined areas that support a variety of learning possibilities for small groups of children; and
• The addition of bleachers to support communication at group meetings.

Visual images of Reggio classrooms have challenged our teachers to rethink some interpretations of principles of good practice. For example, many teachers believe that everything in a classroom must be low and accessible to children. After viewing and reflecting on images of Reggio classrooms, teachers have come to recognize the need to balance this idea with the importance of making classrooms feel more homelike. At home the walls are decorated with objects, pictures, and accessories (often placed out of children's reach) that are not intended to be handled, but are there to reflect interests, values, and the culture of the family.

One unexpected problem related to environments surfaced when teachers first began to emulate the Reggio practice of tape-recording children's conversations. As teachers listened to tapes, they became cognizant of distracting background noise. It became evident that their environments do not support dialogue and serious discussion. In processing this observation, many teachers reflected that they had gone too far in their consideration of the idea that active learning is noisy. They had failed to consider the need for spaces where children and teachers can listen intently to each other and work without distraction. Unfortunately, most schools have little or no space that is protected in this way. Many schools are now struggling to find the resources to renovate space for this purpose.

The concept of the "environment as the third teacher" continues to be developed as we learn to scrutinize every bit of space in our schools. We have begun to realize that this concept is much more complex than any set of guidelines for appropriate equipment, materials, room arrangement, and display. It is tied to our image of the child; knowledge and ongoing study of any given group of children, teachers, and parents; our understanding of the concept of scaffolding; our use of documentation; and our ways of thinking about organization of time and relations among all members of the learning community.

Implications of Slowing Down to Listen

Many teachers comment that as they pursue the goal to listen more effectively to children, they have learned to "slow down." In order to listen, they must spend more focused time with individual children or small groups of children. Often this means changing an established pattern of constant movement from one table or activity area to the next to monitor and facilitate or manage behavior. In reflecting on the need for this kind of change, teachers have recognized that not only had their former pattern of behavior prevented them from listening to children, but it had also inadvertently kept them from modeling focused behavior and perseverance.

Many teachers who wish to slow down must also rethink their values and concepts about equity. For example, several teachers have shared a concern that it may not be fair for a teacher to spend a lot of time with a few children. The implication is that the other children are being neglected. One teacher commented, "I wish I had that luxury." Teachers often operate on a belief that they must be responsive and available to all children at all times. The change toward slowing down, listening to children, and working with small groups forces teachers to deal with the dilemma they feel about equal versus differential allocation of time and resources.

On another level, this same kind of tension and dilemma is experienced when teachers try to move toward a more collaborative approach to teaching. Equitable distribution of work among teachers has often meant equal or same distribution of work. For example, in a room of twenty children and two teachers, each teacher might work with ten children, or each teacher would do the same kind of "floating facilitation" with all the children. Although it would seem to be a simple matter for teachers to reorganize themselves to allow for one to work for an extended and uninterrupted period of time with a small group while the other supervised the larger group, this has not been easy. In situations where teachers are forging new relationships with an *atelierista*, these issues must also be addressed. As one teacher explained, "Personal inter-pretations of shared responsibility vary tremendously." In most American schools, teachers and specialists have worked separately. Team planning, role release, and collaborative decision making mean coordination of work rather than pure division of work. It requires a kind of ongoing negotiation and exchange that is not familiar to most of our teachers.

Slowing down seems to run counter to our traditional value and understanding of productivity. Parents and teachers often equate productivity with how many activities are completed in a day, how much of the curriculum is covered in a given period of time, or how many facts and formulas can be memorized. Teachers who are "slowing down" have learned to value the process of exploring children's ideas, theories, questions, and opinions. They can see that these kinds of interactions with children support positive dispositions toward learning as well as perseverance and depth of learning. They realize that experience must be connected with reflection. One teacher explained that she used to "wow" the kids. She would plan exciting, entertaining, and flashy activities. Each day the children would experience something new. Now, she reflects that these were nothing more than fast-action, fast-paced, superficial experiences. She and her co-teachers have come to look at school as a place for children to pursue their interests, to experience, reflect, construct, and reconstruct meaning from experience. While slowing down seems like a simple change, it requires teachers to reorganize themselves, their time, the environment, and their relations with co-teachers.

Scaffolding versus Interference

All teachers, at one time or another, question whether given interventions help or harm a child. "Should I tell the child the answer?" "Should I show her how to do it?" "Should I ask her to tell me why she chose to use that color paint?" "When are we interfering with a child's creative process?"

Although all teachers will probably always struggle with these kinds of questions, many of our teachers are beginning to learn that they are in a much better position to make these decisions when they take the time to closely observe, listen, and engage in dialogue with children. Through these efforts they are learning to enter the child's world without disrupting or diverting the flow of a child's work or intentions.

Dorris, a teacher of three-year-olds, discovered this when she decided last fall to study how her children approach painting at the easel. She sat next to the children as they painted and then recorded what she saw. She noticed how the children held the brush, how they used it to pick up paint, how they applied paint to paper, where on the paper they chose to begin the painting, what kinds of strokes and movements they made with the brush, how much and what parts of the paper were painted, what the children said when painting, etc. After a short time, the children became curious about what she was doing and asked what she was writing. She shared many of her observations. As a result, the children became involved in talking with her not only about what they did but what effect their actions had on the painting.

What evolved from a simple plan to observe children turned into an opportunity to help children become reflective about their experience.

This teacher learned that close observation can naturally lead to good teaching. She was most certainly scaffolding learning through her close observation and responsiveness to the children's questions and invitations to interact. There was no question in this teacher's mind about whether she was being intrusive or interfering with the flow of a child's creative expression.

Advice from Teachers

Many, many more considerations, interpretations, and difficulties could be shared, and we will continue to process and document these.

This final segment of the paper will highlight a few pieces of advice to teachers who are just beginning their study and implementation of the principles and practices of the Reggio Emilia approach.

1. **Approach old activities in new ways**. One of the reactions to the disequilibrium experienced when old ideas and practices are challenged and new ones are being studied is a feeling of loss and helplessness.

Some teachers describe feeling shaken, anxious, and incompetent. At these times, they need to be reminded that they are not alone. The research on educational innovation and reform tells us that change can be a journey into incompetence. It also tells us that those who have succeeded in adapting or adopting innovations have generally started small, going at the individual's speed and moving at a pace that is comfortable. Change requires time and must be documented to assess effectiveness.

The advice from our teachers who have gone through this stage of concern is to remember that change must happen gradually and be connected to prior learning. One teacher stated, "You must be willing to give up some of your old ways, but be careful not to create a void.

You need to exchange or adapt former methods of teaching."

Here is how two teachers tried to incorporate some of their new understandings from Reggio Emilia with tried, true, and valued activities that had been done with children in years past. They decided to approach their study of the colors, textures, sights, and sounds of fall with some new twists. This time when plans were made for the fall nature walk designed to kick off the study, the teachers planned to take a camera. They had learned that photos and slides of children's observations could be used at a later date to help children revisit and reflect on their experiences. They took pictures of the group walking hand-in-hand down the sidewalk as they ventured out on their walk. They used the camera to capture the children's observations of the beautiful, bright yellows and oranges of the leaves on trees against the sunny sky above. The joy of jumping into a raked pile of leaves was now an image that they could return to again and again. The teachers took a pocket-sized pad of paper to record the children's comments. Later these teachers studied the photos, comments, and dialogue to try to understand the hypotheses and everyday knowledge of the children. By doing this, they were better able to go back to the children a few days later and engage them in discussions about their theories on why leaves fall from trees. They asked the children to help communicate these theories and make their ideas visible by drawing them. The drawings revealed more ideas to discuss and compare.

At another time when the children were painting pictures of fall leaves, the teachers projected slides from the nature walk to help the children re-examine the beautiful colors they wanted to represent.

They also encouraged the children to examine their collections of leaves on the light table. A great deal of conversation emerged about the veins, which one child referred to as the "bones" of the leaves.

Others noticed the change of color that appeared when light was projected behind an otherwise dull-looking fallen leaf. The leaf study, which had in former years been a topic for a few days or perhaps a week, emerged into a long-term investigation that lasted several months and evolved into a project on plants that continued through the spring.

2. **Explore the hundred languages**. Adults and children need to become familiar with the physical properties of different representational media. We are trying to understand the first elements, the simplest rudiments of these media in order to establish an alphabet with which we can communicate and construct knowledge. Teachers have approached this goal in many ways, depending on the resources at hand. Some have drawn upon the expertise of their school's art teacher. Others have ventured into collaborative explorations of paint, clay, or paper with the children. Some, like Dorris, have begun with a study of how young children approach painting. On occasion, we have organized workshops for teachers on using clay and drawing to learn.

3. **Plan for emergent curriculum**. Some teachers, upon first hearing that curriculum in Reggio Emilia is not established in advance, take this to mean that little or no advance planning can be done. It has been very difficult for many of them to learn how to plan for possibilities, to

hypothesize directions for projects, to express general goals, and to plan ways to provoke and sustain children's interest. They recognize that it is important to study the ideas expressed in children's words, drawings, paintings, and play. They know that this will help them learn how to scaffold further learning, but the process of interpreting dialogue and hypothesizing possible lines of a project is often both strange and unfamiliar.

4. **Reconsider time**. We need more time; we need to make better use of our time; we need to think about time in different ways. Many of the issues already discussed are connected to these issues. Collaboration among teachers requires time for group planning, sharing, and reflection. Many teachers feel that insufficient time is built into the work schedule for this. On the other hand, many have come to realize that some of the time that is available for group planning is used inefficiently. Teachers are beginning to recognize the kinds of advance preparation and organization needed for productive group meetings. Perhaps Reggio teachers could help us to better understand how they do this.

5. **Persevere in collaboration**. Collaboration can be wonderful, wearing, and wretched. Our support network has been a delightful source of energy, release, and growth for teachers. Discussion is lively, and ideas flow as we share, reflect, and study together. The wearing and wretched sides of collaboration surface when we try to go further to debate, critique, and coordinate points of view. We find it very difficult to deal with hard critique, let go of ownership of ideas, and question our certainties. This is even more challenging in the daily work setting. Working out relationships based on inter-dependence and mutual respect is quite demanding, to say the least.

6. **Involve parents**. All of the considerations and interpretations already described must be processed with parents. Although all of our teachers have taken some steps to increase family participation and to establish a climate of openness and two-way communication, we have decided that in the coming year we will try to support teachers in learning how to process the Reggio Emilia approach with parents by inviting more parents to participate in the monthly grant group meetings. This will move them into the inner circle of our network and make them true partners in the learning process. We will benefit from the perspective that parents will bring to our discussions.

Conclusion

Our experience underscores what the literature on change process has so clearly stated. We must remember that change can be a journey into incompetence. The individual must be respected, supported, and valued throughout the change process. By creating collegial and collaborative relationships, we support individual and organizational change. We need to provide the necessary resources of time, money, materials, and education. We need to grow in our ability to use conflict as a source of learning. And finally, we need to involve all participants affected by the change.

Appendix

Professional Development Plan

Teacher(s) .... Date..
....
....

Schools ....

1. Selected goal(s):

2. Preferred methods of support for professional development:
(Please circle your choices. If this is a group professional development plan, each person should initial your choices.)
• participation at monthly grant group meetings
• on-site consultation from Louise or Brenda
• peer support group (organized by the grant project or other)
• peer coaching
• team or co-teacher planning and analysis of documentation
• observations at The College School or other schools in the project
• reading
• journaling
• action research or independent study for college credit
• consultation from outside experts
• other (describe in the space below)

3. Evidence/data to be collected through the year to help me/us reflect on progress toward goals:
(e.g., video tape analysis, audio tape analysis, photographic documentation and analyses, journals, child growth measures, behavior performance samples, written or drawn observations of children, written observations and/or critique by colleagues, records of teacher meetings or parent meetings or other communications)

4. Dates on which I/we plan to review and reflect on this professional development plan:

5. What kind of information or resources, beyond those now offered by the Danforth Grant Project, do I/we need in order to successfully implement this plan?

References

COSTA, A.L., R.J. GARMSTON, and L. LAMBERT. (1988). Evaluation of teaching: The cognitive development view. In S. Stanley, and W.J. Popham (Eds.), *Teacher evaluation: Six prescriptions for success*. Alexandria, VA: Association for Supervision and Curriculum Development. ED 299 683.

EISNER, E.W. (1992). Educational reform and the ecology of schooling. *Teachers College Record* 90(4):611 627. EJ 450 826.

FULLAN, M.G. (1990). Staff development, innovation, and institutional development. In B. Joyce (Ed.), *Changing school culture through staff development*. Alexandria, VA: Association for Supervision and Curriculum Development.

FULLAN, M.G., and M.B. MILES. (1992). Getting reform right: What works and what doesn't. *Phi Delta Kappan* 73 (10, June):745 752. EJ 445 727.

FULLAN, M.G., and S. STIEGELBAUER. (1991). *The new meaning of educational change* (2nd ed.). New York: Teachers College Press. ED 354, 588.

HORD, S., W. RUTHERFORD, L. HULLING-AUSTIN, and G. HALL. (1987). *Taking charge of change*. Alexandria, VA: Association for Supervision and Curriculum Development.

VARTULI, S., and B. FYFE. (1993). Teachers need developmentally appropriate practices too. *Young Children* 48 (4, May):36 42. EJ 463 001.

Reggio Emilia:
Its Visions and Its Challenges
for Educators in the United States

Rebecca New
University of New Hampshire - Durham, New Hampshire

We are now at a critical turning point in the decade-long exchange of ideas between American educators and the community of Reggio Emilia. In this paper, I would like to share some of my thoughts regarding the challenges before us.

When I first became aware of the efforts of Reggio Emilia educators early in the 1980s, I was immersed in an ethnographic study of parental values, beliefs, and goals as they influenced patterns of infant care. Throughout my year-long research endeavor in a small working-class community in central Italy, I struggled to make distinctions among three aspects of parental behavior and child development: (1) those that were specific to the community, (2) those that reflected broader Italian norms and values, and (3) those that resonated with parents around the world. I gained much from my first cross-cultural investigation of child care and development. I was reinforced in my conviction that, while there is much that unites our humanness, there are also many dimensions of human experience that are a function of particular circumstances surrounding it, including not only the historical and geographic contexts, but the political, social, and ideological as well. Upon my return to the United States, I gradually began to appreciate *another* benefit of cross-culture research and comparative perspectives on child development. As a result of my struggles to understand how it is that people in one cultural setting make sense of and support children's development, my *own* understandings, beliefs, and values became more self-evident and susceptible to change.

This search for common ground and cultural variation in human interests and behavior has characterized my approach to understanding and *sharing* the work of Loris Malaguzzi and our other Reggio Emilia colleagues. This paper reflects this comparative orientation and is also influenced by my experiences with other early childhood professionals in the United States as we strive to determine the most ethical, equitable, and effective means of caring for the youngest citizens of our society.

What aspects of the work done in Reggio Emilia might assist us in this task? Even as Reggio Emilia faces changes in its political structure and the nature of its citizenship, all would agree that the efforts of the past three decades have taken place in a setting that is relatively wealthy, politically and demographically stable, and ideologically generous. How, then, can lessons learned in this community's early childhood program be transported to the various regions of America, with its political, racial, linguistic, and economic diversity? How can we expect American teachers (in turbulent inner-city schools; in classrooms characterized by increasing numbers of children with developmental, linguistic, and cultural differences; and in communities with little or no support for high-quality child care programs) to emulate what we see in Reggio Emilia? How can we ask teachers to collaborate with parents who are too busy to come to school meetings, to implement long-term projects in the face of growing curriculum demands, to acknowledge and respond to children's many symbolic languages in the face of pressures to emphasize formal academic skills, and to participate in ongoing professional development through the documentation and constant reexamination of their work with children when their contract says the workday ends at 3:15?

I believe that, in order to respond thoughtfully to these questions, we must first be willing to consider the following two questions. First, what aspects of Reggio Emilia are particular to this cultural setting and cannot be transported to another cultural setting? Second, what aspects of the work in Reggio Emilia might challenge us to rethink our American goals and ideals regarding optimal early childhood education? In other words, concomitant to any attempts to implement the Reggio Emilia approach, we must strive to better understand the relationship between our work, our values, and the context of early childhood education in Reggio Emilia and the rest of the world.

Cultural Differences

In my first trip to Italy in 1967, and in all subsequent Italian journeys (many but not all of which have included Reggio Emilia), I have observed varying degrees of the following:
• A strong sense of shared responsibility for children that is expressed at the individual, local, and state levels;
• A belief in the importance of children and families not just as an expression of political sentimentality, but as evidenced through a wealth of formal social policies and informal community and social supports for parents and young children;
• The value of social discourse, often appearing in the form of arguments *(discussions)* in the sharing of opinions and ideas;
• The importance of a certain quality of life, often expressed in the aesthetic details of daily living, including the role of art and design, as well as the presence of good wine and parmesan cheese at the table; and
• The ethic of inclusion as manifest in community social norms as well as educational policies regarding children with disabilities.

Some of these features are as old as the Italian culture itself. Others are the result of more recent concerns and political efforts. They are all interpretations of a civilized society that stand in contrast to the U.S. policies and attitudes. This contrast leads me to consider briefly the historical and political contexts in which teachers in the United States and Italy have operated over the past half century. In postwar Italy, there was a clear and pressing need for the nation to rebuild itself and, in some ways, to redefine the nature of its society. There was a collective struggle to emerge from a fascist self-image to one of a caring and productive society. This struggle is apparent in a variety of literatures, including but not limited to that regarding the women's movement in Italy. The efforts that were begun by Malaguzzi and his colleagues here in Reggio Emilia during that time not only reflected but contributed significantly to that broader movement (New, 1993).

In the United States, there was quite a different national self- image and, as a result, a vast difference in postwar activities on behalf of young children and their families. America had no *apparent* need to rebuild either the social or the physical fabric of society. Neither buildings nor self-image had been wounded, at least in any way that was acknowledged at the time. Rather, Americans felt entitled to gloat, and soldiers returned to their homes as private citizens. Women who had been working in the war-time industry were sent back home to have more babies. Day care centers, many of them of a quality we now envy, were shut down. Child care became, again, a private issue reflecting the broader American cultural value of independence. Today, we continue to struggle with the consequences of that cultural attitude.

In contrast to the American status quo, Italy has changed dramatically over the last half of this century, and Reggio Emilia represents much of what is best about this change. That core of common Italian values, in combination with Reggio Emilia's particular history of collaboration and solidarity, was enhanced immeasurably by the person and the vision of Malaguzzi, who articulated a broader view of children's social, intellectual, and creative competencies than had previously been imagined. Thus we now have the Reggio Emilia preschool system that is world renowned, and much of what intrigues us in the United States about the Reggio Emilia preschools is representative of their particularly Italian dimensions. Yet I am also quite sure that many of us first became interested in Reggio Emilia because it provides such a compelling illustration of *our own* ideals of early education. As others have noted, *we see much common ground* between the work of Reggio Emilia educators and educators elsewhere as we recall, for example,

• John Dewey's challenge to balance the pragmatic with the ideal, to retain a view of the child within society, and to consider the role of school in the restructuring of society;
• Lucy Sprague Mitchell's advocacy of the importance of children doing work with personal meaning and integrity, and the value of the community in providing genuine opportunities for learning;
• Piagetian notions of the child's construction of knowledge;
• Howard Gardner's thesis on our many and multiple intelligences; and
• The implications of post-Piagetian and neo-Vygotskian thought.

Without a doubt, Reggio Emilia acknowledges and expands upon American goals and ideals regarding optimal early childhood education. As we continue in our struggle to use what we already know and believe about learning and development, the Reggio Emilia preschools offer us a much-needed vision of what preschool education looks like when we do it well. Thus, for many, the ability of Reggio Emilia educators to practice what we have often preached will remain their primary attraction.

Yet the work of the Reggio Emilia preschools offers more than confirmation of the more enduring traditions in American early childhood education. Indeed, I believe that the real gift the Reggio Emilia preschools have to offer us is in their role of *provocateur*, which Tiziana Fallopian once explained as *one who gets others to think about something in a new and compelling way*. For example, Reggio Emilia compels us to reconsider the critical nature of a teacher's role in children's learning and development, and the processes by which teachers acquire the competencies about which we now marvel. Let me comment briefly on these two points.

Many aspects of the teacher's role are worth contemplating. Even as we marvel at the extent to which Reggio Emilia children explore topics associated with such content areas as math and science, we remain puzzled by how they determine the content of teaching in Reggio Emilia. It has been stated many times that there is no predetermined curriculum. Rather, children are trusted to be interested in things worth knowing more about; teachers are expected to build upon their knowledge of children *and* their knowledge of the skills and attitudes that are of value in their community as they construct their own environments for teaching and learning. We have much to learn about how teachers acquire this knowledge and negotiate those critical decisions.

Other aspects of Reggio Emilia notions of teaching and teacher development challenge our view as well. In the United States, it is given among professionals in early childhood that well-trained teachers are *essential* to provision of an environment in which children can work together on tasks of significance, share materials and ideas of interest, and respond to challenges and disagreements in an intellectually thoughtful fashion. It is also a given in the United States that teachers will receive the bulk of the necessary training for such a role before entry into a classroom of young children. Notwithstanding some of the more innovative professional development programs going on around the country (through, for example, the Teachers' Institute in Winnetka, Illinois), an unfortunate majority of staff development days in the United States are spent with teachers listening to and participating in someone else's agenda, often seeing little or no relationship to their work back in the classroom.

Italy, on the other hand, has historically required minimal training for early childhood teachers. Any form of inservice training remains dependent on the initiative of individual teachers or regions. As a result, from the outset administrators and town officials in Reggio Emilia have assumed a leadership role in the planning and implementation of teacher training and staff development activities in the ongoing routines of their early childhood program. Further, the way in which the Reggio Emilia teachers use their professional development time reflects a commitment to the belief that adults as well as children need opportunities for sharing, experimenting, revolting, building theory, and constructing knowledge about the world in which they work. Thus the Reggio Emilia interpretation of professional development embraces a conception of teachers as learners and expands upon a model of teaching based upon reflective practice such as that described by Catherine Fosnot (1989). Ways in which this interpretation varies from

U.S. interpretations of teacher development include the processes of deliberate documentation (in the visual as well as the narrative form) of children's experiences and teachers' interpretations of those experiences; an active elicitation of multiple points of view; frequent experimentation, evaluation, and public debate over curriculum decisions; and a continual examination of the social and cultural contexts and consequences of children's schooling.

Yet another way in which the Reggio Emilia approach challenges assumptions underlying American practices of professional development is in the depiction of knowledge. In the United States, it is a given that language is a primary agent in creating and shaping socially constructed knowledge. Teachers in Reggio Emilia seek out variations in the expression of that knowledge as they use children's drawings and photographs, their own sketches of children at work, and other "symbolic languages" to inform their practice. They also acknowledge the need to have an audience in order for that expression to have meaning. Thus they actively engage parents and each other in dialogue around topics of interest and investigation. This emphasis on *collaborative* reflection, in turn, results in outcomes that are expressed in the form of collective understandings. While the U.S. literature on professional development acknowledges the importance of plurality and the need for multiple perspectives, these dimensions rarely characterize actual professional practice. In spite of the fact that, as Maxine Greene (1986, p. 73) so eloquently notes, "the self can never be actualized through solely private experiences," few teachers have access to that "community of inquirers" deemed essential (Killion & Todnem, 1991) to inform and support a teacher's practice.

Thus inquiry-oriented teaching in the United States remains, for many, a lonely venture and may include a "powerful professional loneliness" (Anzul & Ely, 1988, p.682). The notion of such professional isolation would be difficult for teachers in Reggio Emilia to imagine, much less to function in. Teachers in Reggio Emilia are encouraged to think about their work within the context of a stable and supportive network of teachers and *pedagogisti*, some of whom have worked together for more than two decades. In Reggio Emilia, this "community of inquirers" also includes the voices of children's parents, who guarantee the presence of "multiple points of view." In the United States, in spite of the well-established importance of an active partnership between schools and families, few acknowledge the potential role of parents in contributing to teachers' development. The context within which American teachers perform their daily work has been described as a "bleak educational landscape with little engagement with matters of the mind" (Smyth, 1992, p. 275). There is perhaps no better reason to continue in our examination of the Reggio Emilia approach than because it presents an image of the *teacher* as one who enjoys learning as much as teaching, who appreciates questions as well as answers, and who views alternative points of view as opportunities for discussion and observation. The Reggio Emilia approach to professional development provides dramatic illustration of the benefits of enlarging the focus from what works best for children to consider what it is that *teachers* need to inform, improve, and inspire their practice.

Conclusion

Today we have a great concern that American educators will be unable to "retain the magic" of Reggio Emilia's influence on our early educational programs. Our response to this concern must be an emphatic declaration that *it's not magic*. What we've seen in Reggio Emilia is the result of decades of hard work and a commitment to doing what's right by children as well as adults. It's also a *commitment to a process*, meaning that we have to keep asking questions. What we refer to as the Reggio Emilia approach is *not* a formula, it's *not* a quick fix, it's *not* an easily translatable solution for school reform in this or any other country. Carlina Rinaldi once said that there was a danger in referring to Reggio Emilia as a model. I share her concern that what is happening in Reggio Emilia might be viewed as a sequence of steps and procedures that can be emulated simply if someone carefully "follows the directions." There is not only a danger in our desire to emulate what we see in another cultural setting, but even more risk in believing that someone else can discover for us what good teaching is all about. If we believe that the educators of Reggio Emilia can do that kind of thinking and hard work for us, then their influence *will* be ephemeral. Hopefully, however, what we are getting from Reggio Emilia is a passion for a process that acknowledges our need as individuals and as a society to engage in a cooperative learning adventure with others, both children and adults.

The interior walls of the preprimary schools of Reggio Emilia are covered with mirrors. As we see *ourselves* in those reflective surfaces, we will be challenged to think hard about our values, reconsider some of our more cherished beliefs, and reflect more somberly on our goals and practices in early child care and education. That may be the most valuable lesson that we can learn from Reggio Emilia.

References

ANZUL, M., and M. ELY. (1988). Halls of mirrors: The introduction of the reflective mode. *Language Arts* 65 (7, November):685 687. EJ 379 819.

FOSNOT, C.T. (1989). *Enquiring teachers, enquiring learners: A constructivist approach for teaching*. New York: Teachers College Press, Columbia University.

GREENE, M. (1986). Reflection and passion in teaching. *Journal of Curriculum and Supervision* 2 (1, Fall):68 81. EJ 341 170.

KILLION, J.P., and G.R. TODNEM. (1991). A process for personal theory building. *Educational Leadership* 48(6, March):14 16. EJ 422 847.

NEW, R. (1993). Italy. In M. Cochran (Ed.), *International handbook of child care policies and programs*. Westport, CT: Greenwoood Press.

SMYTH, J. (1992). Teachers' work and the politics of reflection. *American Educational Research Journal* 29 (2, Summer):267 300. EJ 449 453.

Different Media, Different Languages

George Forman
University of Massachusetts - Amherst, Massachusetts

Children Learn More Deeply When They Represent the Same Concept in Different Media

Representational media such as drawings made with markers, paper constructions, clay sculpture, and wooden constructions are used in the Reggio Emilia schools to deepen the children's understanding of a theme or concept. Typically, a small group of children will work together in a team, each making a version of his or her idea in several media. In the "Field Project" at La Villetta, one of the schools in Reggio Emilia, the children first talked about a plot of ground outside in their yard, drew what they remembered, made wire and paper models of the ecosystem of spiders, birds, and crickets, and even made noise machines for the sound of rain and of the animals living in the field.
In the project called "The Amusement Park for Birds," a group of children at La Villetta discussed what they knew about water wheels, drew them, and made them in paper, clay, and finally wood and wire. At each passage, their questions about how water wheels work and where they are used deepened and broadened.

Each Medium Has Different Affordances

Now I would like to take a more technical look at the physical properties of various media and how these properties influence thought. Consider the concept "love." How might this concept be represented in blocks or in string? The artist takes the physical properties of the medium into account before beginning to work. Blocks can be stacked, counterbalanced, and arranged in patterns. They fall down if not placed properly. How can these physical properties capture some aspect of love (Figure 1)?
Suppose our artist in residence leans two blocks together and calls the work "Love." The artist presumes that the viewer will interpret this arrangement to mean that "love is a mutually supportive relation." The viewer knows that each of these blocks would fall if not for the other, that these are separate elements each supporting the other. Thus the message of mutual support is both the symbol and the physical property of the medium. With string, again the artist inspects the medium. Strings are flexible, linear, easily curved and tied into knots. The artist decides to tie a small knot in the string and then loop the remaining string into a larger and looser knot that has not been pulled as tightly as the first. This creates a string that has a knot closing onto another knot.

The artist labels this work "Love," and the viewer interprets this to mean that "love can even tie our knots into knots." Each medium has its own set of physical properties, and those physical properties, when inspected by the artist, help to define the message to be expressed. Different media allow the artist to express some meanings more easily than other meanings. The string more easily than the blocks represents the looping of one action on another. The physical properties of the string afford looping. Stated slightly differently, the string possesses an "affordance" for representing the concept of looping.

Fig. 1 Two blocks give each other mutual support

Each medium has physical properties that make some concepts more easily represented than others. The ease of representation is determined by how easily the child can vary a physical property of a medium. Metal can represent a flowing river if it is heated, but I would not suggest that fluidity is an affordance of metal. The transformation of metal from less to more fluid is not easily created; therefore, fluidity is not an affordance for symbolization in this medium. A transformation in the medium that a child can easily produce is an affordance. Each affordance provides the child with a method to express an idea by transforming the medium. Clay is easily twisted; therefore, children can make meaning by using the twist as a symbol, such as showing the anguish in a mouth or the strain of effort in a run. An affordance is the relationship between the transformable properties of a medium and the child's desire to use that property to make symbols.

Each Affordance Provokes a Special Orientation toward the Problem to be Solved

Given that only certain properties of any medium can be varied, children using that medium quickly develop a biased perspective to their work. That is, the medium itself orients children to certain classes of meaning. The medium is not technically the message, but it biases what messages can be easily expressed. Round blocks of wood orient children to dynamic relations, flat blocks to stationary relations, bumpy textures to patterns of light, and so forth (Figure 2).

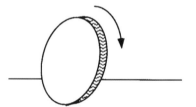

Fig. 2 Round blocks contain dynamic relations

These biases can be considered strengths. This is particularly true if the medium biases children to view the world from an unusual perspective. Take the activity called "The Mime of the Feet," as reported in the Reggio Emilia exhibition *The Hundred Languages of Children*. Here the children decided to act out a story about three people by photographing their feet as the characters.

The children then laid out about sixteen photo-graphs of their feet in various positions to tell the story of a man and woman who are apart at first, get married, dance, are robbed by another character (pair of feet), fight, and then separate because, in the children's words, "When a person fights, it's better to split up, because what's the point of staying on just to fight." I would maintain that the story line was more creative because it derived from the actions that feet afford for symbolization, such as coming together, kicking, and moving apart. The story would have been more conventional had the children used hand puppets. The feet as a medium caused the children to think about a whole different set of relations.

Children Learn to Make Compromises with What the Medium Does Not Easily Afford

Representation also involves an element of compromise between the affordances of the medium and the meaning the child wishes to express. Suppose a child wants to express her concept of elephant, but has only a single sheet of white paper. The paper does not afford her the opportunity to express the attributes of elephant most salient to her. Nevertheless she persists. She tears the paper into the biggest oval that the sheet will allow (Figure 3).

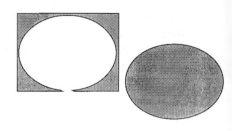

Fig. 3 Child cuts paper into biggest oval possible

Granted, this symbol is completely flat and white, but it has at least captured the largeness and roundness of the child's concept of elephant. Even the symbol for largeness, on some absolute scale, is not large. But since it is the largest oval she can make with this medium the sheet of paper the child is satisfied that the oval can represent the largest land animal she knows.

The child thinks about the referent *elephant* and inspects the physical qualities of the sheet of paper and decides that the paper itself is too small. So she makes the compromise of dealing with the problem at the scale of the sheet of paper rather than at the scale of the real elephant. Thus she makes the largest oval she can, given the constraints of the medium. The child's purpose and use of the medium define its affordances and constraints. The difference between an affordance and a constraint is not physical. A transformable property can be an affordance if it works to carry meaning, but this same property can be a constraint to some other meaning that it does not afford.

The constraints of a medium make it difficult to symbolize certain meanings. The paper used to symbolize elephant has no easy way to cap-ture heaviness or the lumbering walk or the trumpeting roar.

But we need to help children do two things: one, find the best medium for expressing an idea and, two, make creative compromises with the medium at hand. These compromises often yield totally new perspectives on the theme or concept being represented. Furthermore, as I will discuss in a moment, children should learn to traffic between a variety of media. The traffic across media will help children produce new representations informed by old ones, and to revisit and revise these old representations as well.

Other Aspects of Media Affect Representational Bias

Granted, paper can be used to capture the color of the referent by using colored markers, and the human voice can be used to capture the elephant's trumpeting roar. Some media are better suited for chromatic information because they are chromatic; other media are better suited for acoustic information because they are acoustic. The consequences of these media properties are fairly obvious.

For example, a pencil set may or may not vary in color. Take a pencil set with only shades of gray. Such a pencil set would place great constraints on representing the autumn season. But is this affordance interesting or trivial? Granted, if a child could invent a way to portray the four seasons by using only shades of gray, the child's performance would be interesting. But does the contrast between chromatic and achromatic pencils cause us to ask any interesting questions about media? Perhaps not. Media influence representation in ways other than their affordance to changes in color, size, or shape. Media also differ in their modularity, their persistence across time, and the amount of physical feedback they provide. These aspects of media may have more profound effects on representational bias than do their variations in physical properties.

Modularity

Give children a thousand chips of colored paper versus a set of colored pencils. Both media are chromatic, but one is modular and the other, the set of pencils, has no preformed shapes. The pencil medium requires the children to construct the elements by drawing well-defined shapes. Variations in the modularity of a medium place different cognitive demands on the artist, and these differences create different representational biases (Figure 4).

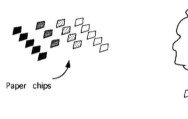

Fig. 4 Chips of paper create their own representational bias

In the above example, a thousand chips of colored paper could create a bias to represent the densely packed colors of fallen leaves. When a medium is modular, that is, when the elements are given, children's attention shifts to the arrangement of those elements. But when the elements are not given, as in a blank piece of paper, the children are biased to representing shapes because this is the first step in making symbols with markers. Indeed, when drawing, children often refuse to overlap their drawn shapes, as if this were a violation of a graphic rule. Every shape has it own encompassing line. To overlap shapes, children would have to violate this rule.

I remember the project called "The Crowd," completed at Diana School in Reggio Emilia. The children were trying to decide why their drawings did not seem to capture the essence of this concept, a crowd. When they drew people in a crowd, each figure drawn was influenced by the previous figure drawn, and the resulting crowd looked too organized and the people too separated. Too many people were moving in the same direction, and every drawn figure had its own right-to-left space. But when the children represented the crowd by using paper doll cutouts of their drawings, they began to experiment with overlapping and with reorienting the passage of people, some facing to the right, some to the left. The affordances of the paper cutouts created a bias to consider the direction of movement and planes in space as couriers of meaning. This was possible because the direction of movement and occlusion for the cutouts was easily transformed.

Persistence across Time

Now let's compare media elements that persist in time versus those that do not. A musical note, once played, is gone. A mark, once made, persists across time. The cognitive demands of making symbols from musical notes places on the child's memory a certain load not encountered with a drawing. In composing music on an instrument, the previous pattern must be remembered. In making a graphic design, the marks persist and are available for repeated review. Given these differences, children will be biased in different ways for each medium. If a child is trying to represent the flight of a bird by using a xylophone, the child is more likely to consider the entire flight path the swoops, rises, dips, and turns (Figure 5). A child who is trying to represent the flight of a bird by using markers is more likely to think about the position of the wings at one moment, then a second moment, and so on. The marks afford this study of successive actions frozen in time, but the xylophone does not. The xylophone is more capable of capturing the changes rather than the positions themselves.

Fig. 5 Markers let the child study successive positions at once

Media That React to Changes

Some media allow children to make more mistakes, and other media are more self-corrective. For example, with paper one can draw an impossible block structure, but with the real blocks one can build only those arrangements that do not fall over (Figure 6).

Media differ in the amount of feedback they provide to children. Thus some media can serve to test an idea, and others can serve to design an idea. I will say more about this difference between design and test later. The distinction between reactive media such as blocks and nonreactive media such as drawing needs further comment. Media such as drawing and painting serve design purposes well because they have more degrees of freedom. With drawing, one can make more complicated shapes and impossible arrangements than one can with reactive media like blocks, which conform to the laws of gravity and friction. However, media such as drawing that best serve the role for design also make the most cognitive demands on children. This greater range of symbolic expression has several effects. First, the child has to invent the shapes and lines because they are not "contained" in the medium.

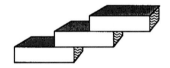

Fig. 6 A drawing allows one to visualize impossible structures

Second, the child has to read these marks as equivalencies to real objects that conform to physical laws. Drawing a round shape that looks precariously balanced requires more graphic literacy than physically trying to balance an oval piece of wood. Thus we have a cognitive dilemma. Drawing as a medium might be best for making a design because it is so open-ended, yet drawing might be the most difficult to read because the physical dynamics of the graphics are virtual rather than real. It behooves us to help children learn to read their graphic designs as virtual embodiments of real physical systems, otherwise their graphic designs will carry no implications for improving the working model. A picture is not automatically a set of instructions. The child has to enter the picture as a virtual system of physical relations, and that is not easy.

Sequences across Media Will Affect the Child's Success

Let us grant that various media, which differ in their affordances, create different representational biases. In what sequence or combinations should we present these media to children? Should children progress through a prescribed cycle of media as they try to understand something? Perhaps it does not matter whether the children draw their ideas first or whether they build them from wood and wire. But with a thoughtful analysis of the affordances of different media, we might decide that different sequences can have very different effects.

Typically, projects in Reggio Emilia begin with what I have termed a type of verbal outpouring, an outpouring of memories, ideas, and speculations about the theme. In the "Amusement Park for Birds," the children began to list the things they remembered seeing in the yard the previous year. They speculated on why birds need houses, why the lake they had made became dirty, how to make a new lake that would stay clear, and what birds might enjoy if the children were to design amusements for the birds.

The verbal medium allows children easy access to their memories. So many of our memories are retrieved through a remembered word, a phrase, and conversation. The spoken language also affords fantasy as well as reality. Under fantasy, I would include all those wonderful theories that children have about how something works, intuitive theories that may never work in the physical world, but that nevertheless have a logic and reasonableness within the confines of their own frame of thought. It is important to begin a quest for understanding by using a medium that allows free rein to thought. Language can be the playground of ideas without being bridled by the universal laws of nature. It is during the verbal outpouring that many of the hypotheses emerge about what could or should be implemented during the project.

As is often the case, during the verbal outpouring, children reach a point where they need to communicate an idea more clearly, either to themselves or to others. They draw their thoughts on paper and then discuss their drawings with their peers. Sometimes the children draw what they know; sometimes through drawing they discover gaps in their knowledge, and often they repair their theories first by changing their drawing and then by adding an oral explanation. Drawing and speaking work together to help the children deepen their understanding.

These drawings can then serve as a plan for making something else. In the "Amusement Park" project, children made drawings of water wheels, then made them in paper while looking at their drawings. The representation of water wheels in words, or we might say the revisiting of one's memories via words, keeps the water wheel concept deeply immersed in a personal and meaningful context. This is the water wheel that saved the fish; this is the water wheel that grinds the flour; this is the water wheel on the mill that I saw with my grandfather.

The power of words keeps the objects contextualized and connected to other meaningful experiences. Given that the water wheel has not been disembodied from these contexts, the children can retrieve these memories later when they try to solve the more technical problems of how a water wheel works (Figure 7).

Fig. 7 The water wheel on a mill adds helpful context

For example, one child told his friends that the water wheel was connected to the side of the mill house. Consider how this context of a water wheel on a mill house must have affected his construction of the paper water wheel. Mentally framing the water wheel as a component of a mill house helped the child make a paper model that would turn when held vertically. Additionally, he also set a flat wheel as his objective, otherwise it could not interface properly with the wall of the mill house. The point here is that the constructed object is always less than the context that generates the object, yet this context gives the final object its rationale. Thus it is extremely important to help young children contextualize their constructions so that the richness of this context can inform the construction. The talking about water wheels, where they are found, what they are used for these memories are brought forward into the drawing, and yet again from the drawing to the paper model.

Children Should Be Encouraged to Revise Earlier Representations because of Later Ones

At this point in the passage from medium to medium, the children working on the water wheels took a more technical stance to their work. How does the water make the wheel go around? Does the water push the wheel or does the wheel push the water? How are the paddles positioned to either push or be pushed by the water? Andrea had drawn a paddle wheel with the paddles in frontal profile. His cardboard model also had the paddles in this orientation. Children will often draw an object and show two different frontal perspectives. The most common case occurs when children draw a house. They draw both the full face of the front and the full face of the side. Andrea had done this in his water wheel drawing (Figure 8).

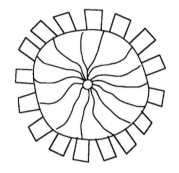

Fig. 8 Andrea drew a paddle wheel with paddles in a frontal perspective

Since Andrea used his drawing as a guide for his paper model, this orientation was brought forward into his cardboard model. Then he set about making his clay model. Clay has an affordance different from that of cardboard. The child can read clay as an object with changeable parts. This affordance sometimes causes children to play with changes even when these changes are not motivated by a particular symbolic intent. They just fool around with the clay. This affordance of changeability is not present in the cardboard. Once the cardboard object is constructed with staples and glue, the components are set. Could it have been the malleability of the clay that caused Andrea to change the orientation of the paddle, perhaps in a playful manner at first, but then as a reflective follow-up? Once the paddle before him was changed, he was provoked to think about the reasonableness of this new orientation. Serendipity plays a big role in problem solving.

Alternatively, it could have been that the clay version was more carefully read as an object upon which water can splash. Once the object-like affordances of the clay were read in this manner, Andrea might have considered, for the first time, the interface between water and paddle. When this image occurred to him, the paddle did not seem right. The interface of water and paddle was not read from the paper model and the drawing because the affordances of these media create a bias toward other aspects the shape of the whole wheel, the story about the fish in the water, the radial symmetry of the spokes coming from the hub of the wheel. But the clay water wheel can be hefted and moved into a stream of water. Therefore, images of the water hitting the paddle blades were more easily provoked by this affordance of the medium. The interesting part of the episode of Andrea's creativity was his desire to return to his paper model and change the orientation of the paper paddle blade. One could expect that this redressing of previous representation could have great benefits. The ultimate benefit would be for Andrea to revisit his pencil drawing of the water wheel and discover that the full view of the paddles was a mistake.

This discovery could have even greater impact on his general understanding of drawing. He could learn how to draw a side perspective of the paddles and, in this discovery, begin to consider in his future drawings whether he had violated rules of good perspective. The intent here is not to teach children how to draw, but to teach them how to read their drawing. It's in reading the drawing that the children can use their drawing to solve problems. Reading the drawing as a guide for action may have little to do with the technical skills of drawing.

Some Media Are Better Suited for
Theory Construction and Others for Theory Testing

It is important to consider the differences between media that help children test a theory and media that allow them to build a theory. Speaking and drawing certainly help children build theories. These media are not constrained by the laws of nature and allow children to play around with ideas until some reasonable hypothesis emerges. Clay and wire and three-dimensional materials have their own spontaneous reactions to the laws of nature (friction, gravity, momentum) and are useful to help children test their theories through simulations.

These media, generally called construction materials, cause the children to place their image into a functional context. Thus a water wheel made from wood and wire will be eyed according to how well it works. Ordinarily a drawing will be eyed according to how well it looks. But hopefully, if a child is drawing in order to build, then the drawing will also be eyed according to how well it represents a working model. It is rather unusual for young children to eye a drawing in order to ask whether it would work if built with construction materials. Such a stance toward a drawing is a case of using a symbol as a guide for action. More commonly, children eye a drawing simply to identify its intended referent, as in, "This is a water wheel on a mill house." The point in using a variety of media is to encourage the children to depart from their usual stance toward a medium. As they traffic back and forth between medium types, the stances toward one should transfer to the other.

We Need to Consider the Child's Level of Media Literacy

To continue this logic, not only would the drawing be eyed as a set of instructions for building a model, but likewise the constructed model could be eyed as the embodiment of a drawing. Once the children learn to traffic in both directions, they become more adept at cycling through the phases of design, test, and design again. Each representation has implications for the other. Both are symbols and referents at various points in this cycle.

We must be careful not to classify media independently of how the medium is used. Certainly drawings can be used to test a theory, at least in the hands of someone who is literate in graphic conventions and who can mentally navigate the implications of a technical drawing (Figure 9). In fact, the U.S. Department of Patents does not require a working model to establish the value of an invention. A drawing is sufficient. However, for young children, we should not assume this level of literacy. It serves us better to recommend construction materials for theory testing and drawings for generating the relevant questions to be tested.

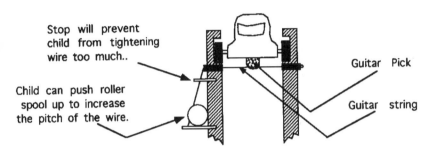

Stop will prevent child from tightening wire too much..

Child can push roller spool up to increase the pitch of the wire.

Guitar Pick

Guitar string

Fig. 9 U.S. patents rely on drawings, even without physical models

We Need to Accept the Partial Theory as if It Were Complete

A special digression is needed here to qualify what I mean by "working model" or "simulation." I do not advise that we encourage children to build a working model of a water wheel or an elevator for birds, at least not in any completed form. I have seen too many cases where children are asked to build an apparatus that really works or that meets adult standards for strength and safety. Once we ask children to enter this world of the adult standard for functionality and safety, we will lose the enterprise for the children. Thus, in the "Amusement Park for Birds," it was not important that the elevator door did not open, or that the elevator could not stop during its ascent. The elevator was simply a feathered box on a pulley cord. Yet in their attempts to make a working model, the children were learning about inverse relations: pulling down makes something go up. And they were confronting what this simple machine did not have that a better elevator would have. The simulation may give answers to some subset of questions, but it also has value as a vehicle for generating new questions.

Summary

• Children learn more deeply when they represent the same concept in different media.
• Each medium has different affordances.
• Each affordance provokes a special orientation to the problem to be solved.

• Children learn to make compromises with what the medium does not easily afford.
• Other aspects of media, such as modularity, persistence across time, and amount of feedback affect representational bias.
• Sequences across media affect the child's success.
• Children should be encouraged to revise earlier representations because of discoveries made with more recent representation.
• Some media are better suited for theory construction and others for theory testing.
• We need to consider the child's level of media literacy.
• We need to accept the partial theory as if it were complete.

Staff Development in Reggio Emilia

Carlina Rinaldi
Municipal Preprimary Schools of Reggio Emilia - Reggio Emilia, Italy

In schools like ours in Reggio Emilia, which consider relationships and interaction as the nuclei of the education of young children and propose research as a permanent learning strategy for both children and adults, we must ask ourselves: What new meanings does the term *staff development* take on? This term, like many others, must be redefined to distinguish it from old stereotypes that derive from pedagogical practices dating back to old courses of study. These courses, in spite of their various differences, often attempted to pour ideas into teachers, to shape them, so that they could in turn shape the children according to prespecified objectives. In this way, everything seemed clear-cut, clean, predictable, and prepackaged. The results were guaranteed or at least they were thought to be. But this method had little to do with research, reflection, observation, documentation, doubt, uncertainty, or true education. Above all, it didn't consider the most important aspect of education *the child* as much as we believe it should.

Good staff development is not something that is undertaken every now and then, reflecting only on the words of someone else. Instead, it is a vital and daily aspect of our work, of our personal and professional identities. Staff development is seen above all as change, as renewal, and as an indispensable vehicle by which to make stronger the quality of our *interaction* with children and among ourselves.

Staff development then becomes seen as a *right* of each individual teacher and of all teachers within the school. In fact, it is the right of every individual within a group and of the group as a whole working *together.*

To be in a group creates a new collegial dimension in the school. This colleagueship of teachers as a cohesive unit creates a new subject, a new protagonist and, as a unit, has a right to particular working conditions: the right to think, to plan, to work, and to interpret together. In fact, a new concept of didactic freedom emerges as the right to discuss and challenge ideas, to have an *interactive* collegial relationship.

The group is not characterized simply by the sum of individual thoughts of individual people or as a game between minority and majority thinking. Instead, it is a new way of thinking, it is a co-construction *together* towards a common interpretation of educational goals. Each teacher, therefore, has individual rights, but also rights pertaining to the group. The most important right is to be able to work closely with children, colleagues, and parents on the practical and organizational level. In our view, staff development as both an individual and a group right assumes the following dimensions.

The Guarantee of Daily Working Conditions

Working conditions referred to here are those that enable the practices of listening, observing, and doing research and documentation, all of which are essential for an authentic interaction with an individual child and with a group of children. This is not only a matter of organization but also an ethical issue.

• In terms of the environment, it means a space that is well thought-out and also pleasant, a space where one can act and work well with children.

• It means a child-adult ratio that allows true relationships and sharing of experiences to be established with children and among children over time; that is, to create together complete narratives rather than short episodes.

• It requires two teachers, present at the same time with the same group of children on a long-term basis that is, over the course of the whole day, the week, the year, and even over several years, *always together*. In our experience, two teachers working together are needed in every classroom in order to observe and interpret from different points of view those active processes that children use to construct knowledge. Two teachers are needed also to document those processes, to interpret them, and to use them as clues in designing the next step of a project. (These are the essential elements that identify the role of the teacher.) All of this allows involvement in projects and in choice making in the daily work, which is characterized by obser-vations and interpretations, which in turn are ever-changing, thanks to the actions and reflections of the children and adults together.

Time and Space

The "trafficking" of ideas and experiences mentioned above is essential, but more is needed. A time and place must be set aside not just daily, but also weekly, in which the interpretations, hypotheses, and doubts that the pair of teachers has constructed can be discussed with and enriched by their other colleagues. In the Reggio Emilia schools, every week the school staff meets to engage in a dialogue about the project in each classroom. Given that the group is formally gathered together, a wider range of issues that are connected to the running of the institution is also discussed: possible meetings with parents, with the community, and with other schools. Time is therefore fixed within the work schedule for these meetings (two and a half hours per week). The meetings are held at 4:00 p.m. when most of the children's activities are over. The adults choose a suitable meeting place according to the equipment they will be using videos, tapes, books, or files. Furthermore, there is a daily habit of exchanging ideas and reflections. This informal exchange is just as rich as the formal meetings because it allows for communication about the processes and their progress.

Parent Participation

Meetings with parents represent another important form of staff development not easy, but very important. We have abandoned those formalized rituals characterized by descriptive language or, worse, by evaluative language. Instead, we have created parent meetings that are no longer individual in nature, but involve the entire group of parents of one classroom. The aim of these meetings, with the aid of documentation, is to show and share the processes, the theories, and the insights of the children with the parents. At these meetings, the abilities of all the children are commented upon and explained. We do not comment as is usually the case on the performance of one particular son or daughter. Comparing different cultural or subjective points of view, listening to different opinions, and coming to agreement are valuable not only as parts of a newly characterized professionalism, but also because, from this process, the profession becomes better qualified and defined.

Competence

The fundamental premise of staff development is that it will develop the competence of the teacher by fostering interaction with children, parents, and colleagues. Moreover, every child has the right to have a competent, well-informed teacher. This competence is acquired through practice and through reflection within the teacher group. We also believe that it is essential for the teachers in our schools to be competent in other fields. Teachers should be well educated in the broadest sense of the word. The teacher ought to be a person belonging to our present-day culture who, at the same time, is able to criticize, to question, and to analyze this culture. The teacher ought to be intellectually curious, one who rebels against a consumeristic approach to knowledge and is willing to build upon knowledge rather than to consume it. To consider the teacher as such is both a premise and an objective.

Staff development can be organized in such a way that it brings together men and women from all walks of life who are looking for new meaning and new values both within and beyond the conventional boundaries of thought. It can include interdisciplinary encounters with scientists, biologists, architects, directors, musicians, poets, and the like who, in addition to sharing their specific knowledge, can share with us their worlds and their learning processes. It is up to us to interpret and adapt this information to our own needs.

All of this makes sense and adds to our professional competence if we are aware of it and if we put it into practice. In fact, our main job is to facilitate the entrance of children into the culture and the symbols around them and to help them to *create new cultures and symbolization* while respecting their own personal strategies, their own ways, their own timetable. The children are competent in this regard. We must support their "journey" by building with them and for them a network of understandings that is founded on the continual intertwining of the fields of knowledge and the fields of experience.

What do we mean by fields of knowledge and fields of experience?

Fields of knowledge represent the cultural symbol systems around which a child's first moments of socialization occur. They represent the entry into organized knowledge related to the school. (The word "field" is intended almost in the sense of a magnetic field, a zone of attraction in which elements converge and nourish one another. Thus we can speak of linguistic or mathematical "fields of knowledge.") As an example, one field of knowledge that is of great fascination to most children is that of spoken and written language (words and symbols).

The desire to know language, to decode it, and to use it is very strong in almost every child. Children need not so much to be helped to recognize letters and to compose words, but above all to recognize and sustain their own evolution in the use of language. They need, therefore, to appreciate language as a means of communication. They need to discover that by using this symbol system (written words) they can modify a situation by putting forth an idea, or simply a specific desire, for example, by sending a written message inviting a friend to play. This example can apply to all other fields of knowledge defined as symbol systems that are also powerfully connected to one another. We distinguish them only in functional terms: space, order, and measurement; time, things, nature; body and movement; speaking and words; messages, form, media; self and others.

The problem is not so much to question ourselves about *how* to teach children, but to ask ourselves *what* and *how* children can learn *from* a certain situation. It is necessary to construct, based on the synergy of these fields of experience, educational situations that are truly significant for both the child and adult; to construct situations in which individual children can find not only an understanding of the specific topic, but also an understanding of their own learning style and a deeper understanding of themselves.

Fields of experience are thus the wishes, demands, curiosities, and hypotheses that the children put forth in their journey through the fields of knowledge. Their desires become apparent when the children ask the adults to listen to, observe, and support them and to render them visible. To render them visible means that their processes should be carefully recorded, transcribed, reflected upon, and *respected and sustained*. They may ask the teachers to abandon the set program, the prescribed curriculum, and the usual obligatory courses, and then to join with them in exploring something else. The teachers must therefore keep a clear map of the cultural symbol systems in their head and of how these systems are continually expressed and transformed. At the same time, the teachers must never lose sight of the procedures, the road, the particular way that children organize their behavior or their ideas in order to take hold of a "piece of the world and of life".

The map of ideas that is built in this way represents an essential element for producing a sense of orientation and choice, using sensitivity, experience, and culture. The metaphor is that of a journey into unknown territory where a compass is the most useful instrument. The feelings belong to the children: curiosity, wonder, enthusiasm for the unknown. The courage necessary for this journey lies in the courage to choose, to make mistakes, and to be uncertain.

The result, at least the most obvious one, is the discovery of a new sense of freedom, sociability, and solidarity among both children and adults.

An Integrated Art Approach in a Preschool

Giordana Rabitti
Instituto Regionale per la Ricerca,
Sperimentazione e Aggiornamento Educativi (IRRSAE)
(Regional Institute for Educational Research, Experimentation
and Inservice Teacher Training) Emilia Romagna, Italy

*Editor's Note: This paper is based on the author's 1992 Master of Arts thesis,
"Preschool at La Villetta," at the University of Illinois at Urbana-Champaign.*

Overview

The Setting: The Reggio Preschools

The municipal preschools in Reggio Emilia, Italy, have developed a
particular pedagogical approach, increasingly known around the world
as the Reggio Emilia approach. A traveling exhibit, *The Hundred
Languages of Children*, which has been touring Italy and abroad,
depicts the complexity of the experience and the richness of the
children's products. For a long time and increasingly in the last four to
five years, these schools have captured the interest of international
educational experts such as Howard Gardner, David Hawkins, and
Lilian Katz. Many excellent publications have been printed on the
subject.

Chance brought me into contact with the Reggio preschools. I was born
in that town in northern Italy and have lived there all my life; there too I
worked as a teacher of English for twenty years. Since 1985, I have been
working at IRRSAE-Emilia Romagna.[1] In 1989, I had the opportu-nity
to enroll in the master's degree program in education at the Univer-sity
of Illinois at Urbana-Champaign. As partial fulfillment of the requirements for my degree, Dr. Robert Stake, my graduate adviser, suggested I
conduct a case study of the Reggio schools, with a focus on art.

The educational institutions run by the Reggio Emilia Municipality are
both infant-toddler centers and preschools; there are twenty-two
preschools and thirteen infant-toddler centers. All of these schools
share the same educational philosophy. Some of them, such as Diana
and La Villetta,[2] serve as outstanding examplars of this rationale.

The director of the schools assigned to me the school named La Villetta
as the site for my research. Since my first visits, I had the feeling that
focusing on art might provide too narrow a point of view.

---

[1] Instituto Regionale per la Ricerca, Sperimentazione e Aggiornamento Educativi
(Regional Institute for Educational Research, Experimentation and Inservice Teacher
Training), funded by the Italian Ministry of Education.

[2] The names in this paper have not been changed.

While foreign visitors often associate these schools with art,[3] the staff never uses the word art in discussing their work with the children. What is heard more and more around the school is "project work." Pictures taken of children engaged in a project hang on the walls, transcripts of conversations with children before and during a project are pinned on wood panels, drawings that are parts of a project are displayed in the classrooms everywhere evidence of projects can be seen. *Project* is a key word used by the staff; nobody speaks of art, unless specifically on the subject. Where does this apparent discrepancy between what outsiders see and what insiders say come from?

The staff advocates that project work reflects their idea of schooling as a holistic process that should address "a child's need to feel a whole,"[4] with an integration of all activities. On the other hand, the schools have a feature that distinguishes them from all other preschools in Italy: *atelier* (art studio, a place devoted to the development of visual and graphic arts) and an *atelierista* (a specialized art teacher).

How the educators use a specialized person and specialized place to accomplish this general educational aim seemed to me a problem worth investigating in my thesis, where I stressed the operational curriculum (Goodlad, 1979). My questions concerned how staff and children act in the atelier and in the classrooms, what links exist between projects and daily activities, how these beautiful products are accomplished, what the creativity-skills relationship is (Gardner, 1989), how the environment is set (Elkind, 1987), what the relations with parents are, what idea of art project participants share, and which "expressive languages" they favor. My thesis also covered general aspects of the school program.

Purpose of the Paper

On rereading my thesis, I was struck by how physically scattered in the school the traces of a project are. I thought it could be interesting to follow these tracks as evidence of the integration of the approach espoused by the school. By pondering how projects are started and carried out and by probing the staff's opinion on art and childhood, I have reached a deeper understanding of some of the pedagogical implications of the Reggio Emilia approach to preprimary education.

Methods

I used a naturalistic case-study method (Stake, 1978; Stake et al., 1991), concentrating my attention mainly on one school, La Villetta. The case-study method is particularly responsive to the situation and attentive to the meanings and perceptions of all the people involved.

In line with this approach, I collected data through the following:

---

[3] A typical question posed by visitors is: "How many of your former pupils have become artists?"

[4] Comment 4 in the "commentary" of the exhibit, *The Hundred Languages of Children* (Department of Education, 1987).

• Repeated observations of the activities in the atelier and in the classroom. For my thesis, I visited the school twenty times and stayed for full school days from 8:30 a.m. to 4:00 p.m. and three mornings from 8:30 a.m. to 1:00 p.m. I also attended four different types of staff-parent meetings, three inservice training sessions, and one school board meeting.
• Formal and informal interviews with school staff and all those involved with the schools.
• Analysis of the material (published material, children's work and portfolios, series of pictures, slides, documentation of the work in the school archives).

After completing my thesis, I kept in touch with the schools and all those involved with them. I met them on various occasions, attended public meetings with delegations of foreign educators, and took some groups to visit the schools.

Tracking A Project: The Wind Machine

On my first visit to La Villetta, I was taken around the school by one of the teachers, Amelia Gambetti, who wanted to familiarize me with the environment before my class observations. When we came to the *atelier*, Giovanni Piazza, the *atelierista*, directed my attention to a big white plastered structure, "The Wind Machine." The name rang a bell in my mind; I remembered having seen some children's drawings on a panel with the same name hanging on the wall in the four-year-old class. The computer-generated title of the panel read: *The Wind Machine: a machine for the air and the wind, to fly birds, airplanes, helicopters and the balloons.*
The project that was being carried on in the *atelier* had, in fact, originally started in the four-year-old class. The topic, "the wind machine," came out during a conversation with the teachers on the children's return from the gym, which is outside the school. The children described a game they had played in the gym: they had to direct some balloons, moving them on the floor by blowing them so as to reach a particular line. During the conversation, a child who was probably tired of blowing had claimed he could invent a machine to blow balloons; some other children took up his idea. During my visit, the conversations the first and those that followed during the project were transcribed and displayed on the classroom walls next to the children's drawings. (See Appendix 1.)
The teachers liked the children's idea, discussed it with Giovanni Piazza, the *atelierista*, and together decided to offer the group of interested children[5] the chance to build the machine. The process was long and included (a) drawings based on the conversations, (b) analysis of the drawings, (c) discussion of the materials named in the conversation to be used in the machine, (d) sharing of the project with the families, (e) search for the materials inside the school and at home,

[5] The children who finally worked on the wind machine project were Alice, Filippo, Giorgia, and Simone, two boys and two girls.

(f) construction of the wood structure, (g) gluing of paper to the structure, and (h) decoration of the structure. Slides were taken throughout the whole process and carefully filed by Giovanni to document the work.

The Activities during the Project

The scattering of the traces of the project appear to me to reflect the integration of places (gym, classroom, *atelier*, children's homes), teachers (gym teachers, classroom teachers, *atelieristi*, *pedagogisti*), children's activities (conversations, drawings, building, projects, decorations, cooperation, discussions), and times. The project in fact took several months to complete. I was told by the teachers, and it was confirmed by my observations, that everything and everyone rotated around the children who had the first idea and the subsequent ideas that evolved as the work progressed. What I particularly want to stress is that during one single activity of the project many opportunities were caught and activated by the teacher(s): some of the activities were obviously learning opportunities, others do not appear like that at first sight; some might be seen as "artistic," others do not seem to belong to the realm of art.

When I started my investigation at La Villetta, the children who had planned the Wind Machine had already built the structure, plastered it, and decided on the decoration. At the point when my observations began, they were decorating the machine, which was placed in the *atelier*. They were deeply involved in their work, each one active in the part he or she had negotiated with the group. The children had to follow the individual project that each of them had drawn and that the *atelierista* had placed near them.

As I mentioned before, I saw children decorating the machine, but engaged in many other related activities as well. Early in the course of their work, the children had to move a heavy ladder. It took a long time and it was problematic for them. I was silently wondering why the teacher did not move it himself, when the atelierista, as if reading my mind, explained that "we do every step, as the children are not used to dealing with such big things" (Rabitti, 1992, p. 48). Later on, he claimed that the moving of the ladder, with the different "orders" the children gave each other "Go straight on," "Turn right," "Not that way!" and so forth was as important as the actual building of the machine. Actions of this kind activate social and language skills and communicative exchanges that "socialize problems of statistics, measurement, logic, mathematics, which are no longer abstract concepts, but real problems, full of meanings and highly motivating" (Rabitti, 1992, p.93).

While working, the children were stimulated by the teacher to reason about colors:

Now Giorgia asks for the color green. Giovanni pours the color into the airbrush and remarks, "Here it is; as green as grass." From his perch, Filippo objects, "Grass is dark green; that is light green." "And can't it be grass?" asks Giovanni. Filippo mitigates his assertion, "Light green is the grass that the sun doesn't touch." (Rabitti, 1992, p. 35)

1. On returning from a morning in the gym, the teacher and children revisit the morning's events, remembering and discussing their experience together. Among the various activities in the gym, it seems that the children's least favorite was blowing on balloons to keep them up in the air, and the question is raised whether or not to continue this game during the subsequent mornings... perhaps they need to think of something else to do.

2. Other ideas are added to Giorgia's. So the desire to build a machine that can blow the balloons is consolidated, and the children decide to make graphic representations of their ideas so that they can better illustrate them to their friends.

3. Giorgia is drawing her machine:
"I'm making the rainbow in the sky that's up high, up there with the wind. Then I'm going to make a thing like a fan. I have one at home that blows real hard".

4. The children then need to choose one design, among the many ideas proposed, to try out in three dimensions. How to decide? The criteria they identify is to choose the design that seems the easiest to actually carry out because it has the most details. The children are enthusiastic about really building the machine, so the decision is soon made: Stefano's project will be the one to be constructed.

5. *Proceeding with their plans, the children discuss and compare ideas on the actual constructive possibilities of the materials they have chosen. They proceed by trial and error. Assembling the materials is difficult, and they call in Giovanni, the atelierista, to help. Giovanni lends them his skill by helping them to connect certain pieces together.*

6. *Once this problem has been resolved, the excitement spreads. Large-scale construction requires the children to join their forces in a synergy of purpose and cooperation.*

7. *The children soon realize, however, that the original drawing, being two-dimensional, did not account for the three-dimensionality of the object, so they have to go back to drawing. The basic structure of the machine in wood is drawn again from multiple points of view and re-conceptualized in its entirety. Then the various constituent parts of the machine are redesigned in the new drawings.*

8. *Following the children's discussion on their new graphic representations, certain constructive aspects still need to be clarified. New materials such as paper and cardboard, proposed to the children by the teacher, seem to be ideal for helping them arrive at the right solutions.*

9. The children then test their various hypotheses in three dimensions, in this case using cardboard.

10. The teacher and the atelierista discuss the possible solutions identified by the children. They decide to suggest that the children make a comparison between their hypotheses and then work together, children and adults, to decide on most suitable solutions.

11. The discussion proceeds and ideas are streamlined. The final choice of the design is made, and the material for building the bearing structure of the machine is chosen. Wood and wire mesh will be used for the "skeleton" to which sheets of paper will be glued.

12. Working from higher up changes the point of view, creating new relationships and leading to modifications of the original design.

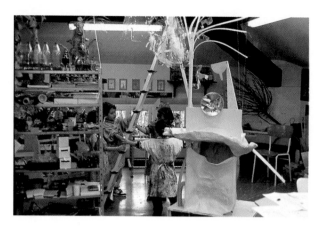

13. The filled and empty spaces, the light and shadow that play on the structure of the machine confirm the feasibility of the design and suggest new possible interpretations. The color rests on the shapes, redesigning the contours and reconfirming the meanings attributed.

14-15. The three-dimensional models in paper serve as anchors for the children's memory of the ideas they had previously worked out together.

16-17. Giorgia and Alice decorate the wind machine. The pleasure, the joy, the awareness of really creating their machine is reinforced through the use of an airbrush that gives shape and color to the air.

18. Small "found" motors brought from home produce an artificial wind that keeps the balloons aloft. The children now have the final reward, the significance of their working together to reach their objective.

20. The parents were constantly informed and involved during the project, and the experience is discussed during a final meeting in which the teachers describe the problems that arose and the strategies that the children found for solving them during the process.

19. The wind machine.

The children were also invited to think about materials and their different characteristics and possibilities:

[Simone] asks the teacher for a piece of paper of a different color. Giovanni hands him the paper and asks the boy: "Are the two pieces of paper the same, I mean this one and the one I gave you before?" Simone touches it, "This one scratches, that one doesn't." Giovanni (rubbing the paper), "And this makes this noise... what about that one? Are they different?" "Yes." Giovanni insists, "If you pull this one, it gets longer." "And this one, does it get longer?" "No." Giovanni agrees, "Good. Now we'll use this paper to make the things to stick up here, O.K.?" (Rabitti, 1992, p.51)

I saw the children add realistic details. For example, when Filippo was working on the speedway that he had wanted in the Wind Machine having observed that there was always a lot of wind in his father's open car when he speeds up on a speedway he had the sudden inspiration to build a tollgate as well:

"I'm thinking how I can make the tollgate..." he wonders as if speaking to himself. Giovanni asks him what a tollgate is. "What you press and the ticket comes out," is the concise answer. The teacher invites him to have "A look over there; there are many small boxes... maybe they will do." (Rabitti, 1992, p.55)

At the same time, I saw the children's nonrepresentative art being acknowledged and respected:

Alice is admiring Giorgia's work large red spots "But, Giorgia, they look like fires!" Giorgia, very seriously, "Exactly! That's what they are: fires." Giovanni too is admiring Giorgia's work, "How wonderful! Do you like it, Alice?" And he adds to me, "They work a lot on abstract art." (Rabitti, 1992, p. 55)

This complex work and all the different tracks of a project find a unity first in the teachers' minds and then in the final project. The staff regularly hold inservice teacher training sessions and discuss the whole process of a project in detail.[6]
At the end of the project, the product is shown in the school, and its story is neatly documented in the archives. An example of this is Giovanni's summary of the Wind Machine project in Appendix 2.

Framework and Perspectives

The Reggio Approach

My tracking of the Wind Machine seems to me to epitomize the Reggio approach. To describe it, I would like to quote Gardner (1993):
It is a collection of schools for young children in which each child's intellectual, emotional, social, and moral potentials are carefully

---

[6] The term, in detail, means dealing also with such minute aspects of the work as the formation of the group, the size of the sheets of paper, etc.

cultivated and guided. The principal educational vehicle involves youngsters in long-term engrossing projects, which are carried out in a beautiful, healthy, love-filled setting. Dewey wrote about progressive education for decades but his school lasted a scant four years. In sharp contrast, it is the Reggio community, more so than the philosophy or method, that constitutes Malaguzzi's[7] central achievement. Nowhere else in the world is there such a seamless and symbiotic relationship between a school's progressive philosophy and its practices. (p. x)

This passage grasps the core of the Reggio schools, their integrated educational action. The children's beautiful projects may mislead outsiders to think of the schools as "art schools," but art is not the school mission. When a project and the daily routine are investigated, however, art reappears. But which concept of art?

Definition of Art

Where does the school stand with respect to various approaches to art education in schools advocated by leading art experts? The main approaches consist of a mixture of production of and reflection on art; differences occur in emphasis on one or the other. On the American scene, greater emphasis on production is voiced, for example, by Gardner (1989); while the Getty Projects, based on the writings of Broudy (1972) and Eisner (1985), emphasize production, perception, and reflection. On the Italian scene, a mixture of production and reflection is manifest in both Bernadoni (1988) and De Bartolomeis (1990).

All of the above approaches emphasize the importance of art and aesthetic experiences for critical thinking in general; all of them, anyway, see art as a separate part of the curriculum. On the contrary, what seems to me to characterize the approach of the Reggio Emilia preschools is their concept of art. All educational statements made in school documents or in presentations at conferences, answers to questions on the topic of art, and observations of school life that I made are in agreement and can be summarized by this statement of Giovanni: *Art means to have more languages and more languages mean different ways of looking at the world. It means the skill to "defamiliarize" situations, daily events as well as objects... look at the different representations of the [same] objects around the school, such as the dandelions downstairs... We would like our children not to stop at the first impression: we want them to have more images of one thing, a wealth of images. (Rabitti, 1992, p. 20-21)*

I found echoes of a similar definition in a well-known novel:
"I suppose not," Philip admitted. "Habit ruins everything in the end, doesn't it? Perhaps that's what we're all looking for desire undiluted by habit."

[7] Loris Malaguzzi was the charismatic leader of the Reggio Approach. He died in January, 1994.

"The Russian Formalists had a word for it," said Morris.
"I'm sure they did," said Philip. "But it's no use telling me what it was, because I'm sure to forget it.
"Ostranenie," said Morris. "Defamiliarization. It was what they thought literature was all about. 'Habit devours objects, clothes, furniture, one's wife and fear of war... Art exists to help us recover the sensation of life'. Viktor Shklovsky." (Lodge, 1991, p. 80-89)

Agreement on this definition of art leads us to understand why we do not need to purposely teach art to lead children to create such beautiful products. As Malaguzzi claims:
Art is learned outside art: I mean, you do not learn how to draw by drawing only. Of course you do need to learn techniques, but you learn how to draw as well by doing other things... and conversely you learn math also by planning and building... Art wears everyday clothes, not Sunday's best. (Rabitti, 1992, p. 112)

Concepts of this kind made Malaguzzi want to have an *atelier* and *atelierista* in the school. In this way he complicated life for children, teachers, and parents by introducing "new languages" (visual arts) into a school mainly based on language arts and social skills.
And we can reasonably infer that the more "new languages" (music, dance, drama, etc.) we introduced, the richer school life might get. Didn't Malaguzzi dare to entrust children with "the hundred languages"?

Conclusions: Educational Significance

I started by observing that *project* is a key word in the Reggio schools. In fact, project work seems to be the answer that the preprimary schools of Reggio Emilia have found to their commitment to address the whole child by offering an integrated educational approach. Inasmuch as the term *project* is widely used in educational research and practice, I close by indicating what the Reggio Emilia schools mean by project, using the school's own definition. The following quotation is taken from a school presentation of a project titled "The Shadow Play":
Is it possible to build a project mainly related to the interests and curiosities of children, in an attempt to investigate and discover their own methods, the development of their ideas, words, graphic representations, and play? Is it possible that investigating where shadows come from and how they change can hold children's attention for a long time?

After my experience at La Villetta I feel I can answer affirmatively: it is possible, if adults share the belief of the importance of critical thinking and metaphoric imaging and believe that children have these abilities. If adults believe it, then they can respect the following:

• The environment is neatly and carefully prepared and set to collect and show the "memories" of children's personal and collective work.
• The teachers act as "memories" of children's activities and projects.

- The teachers think it is important to carefully listen to the children and they know how to do so.
- The teachers are ready to accept the children's ideas and to facilitate the implementation of those ideas.
- The teachers know a lot about materials and skills and know how to present them to the children.
- The teachers know how to work together.
- The teachers know how to provide situations in which children can work together.
- There is both organization and flexibility in carrying out the work.
- Creativity and skills are activated in a mutual exchange.

All of this happens in the Reggio Emilia preschools; I think it should happen at other levels of schooling and in other places as well. And it is possible, if there are a lot of ifs a key feature is present, that of well-planned inservice training through which the staff come to share pedagogical values and carefully discuss their own daily work.

Appendix 1: The Children's First Conversation

November At school, back from the gym: "Verbal Reconnaissance" (ricognizione verbale)

Filippo: In the gym running is great fun ...
Simone: And jumping on the spring-board (?)...
Giorgia: And balancing on the wooden bench (?)...
Alice: And tagging (chasing each other) and... marching...
Simone: Yes... but it's really a drag blowing balloons on our knees...
Filippo: I never win, and then my knees hurt a bit...
Ilaria: And my hands...
Simone: Hey, guys, if we invented a machine to blow balloons?
Giorgia: And who can do it?
Filippo: We can ask Amelia [one of the teachers] how to do it...
Alice: To make a machine we need some wind, and where can you get it?
Filippo: I don't know!
Simone: And you, Amelia, you know how to build a machine to blow balloons?
Amelia: I might think about it, but we might ask Giovanni as well if hehas some ideas...
Filippo: Yes, we may ask him...
Alice: Yes, Giovanni has so many things in the atelier...

In the *atelier*, with Giovanni, Amelia, and the group of children.

Amelia: Giovanni, the children have something to ask you; they
would   like to know... true, Simone?
Simone: Er... er... yes, we would like to build a machine, a machine which can blow balloons...
Alice: Which can spit the wind...
Filippo: In the gym they make us blow balloons; who reaches the
wall   first he wins...
Giorgia: And we are fed up...
Ilaria: We would like to build a machine which blows the balloons, so we don't do it any longer!
Giovanni: But do you have any idea about how to build a machine which can blow the balloons?
Simone: Well, for me it takes a strong wind which pushes the balloons a wind like the one in the sky...
Giorgia: Or like a ventilating (?) fan...
Filippo: The machine must be some (?) big...
Simone: As big as a little hillock...
Giorgia: As a rainbow which is held up there by the wind...
Simone: The machine can be like a big chimney where instead of smoke the wind comes out...
Ilaria: You say like a tower...
Filippo: Maybe like a tall tower...
Alice: Like a sculpture...

Giorgia: Like the Color Tower there [a sculpture in the atelier]...

Simone: No, guys, not that big... who can do it? It touches the roof...

Filippo: We need to make a drawing... which is a project to know how we can do it...

Giovanni: If you, Filippo, already have an idea, you can take a sheet... if you want... the size you need, and can try to draw your machine...

Simone: Me too, I have an idea and I want to draw it... I make a tall tall tower... which the wind comes out, better a big wind...

Filippo: I'll try, but I do not know if I can... May you help me, if I need it, Giovanni?

Giovanni: Certainly. I am really curious to see what these machines which blow balloons look like...

Giorgia: I try too; I'll make the rainbow in the sky which stays up there with the wind, as the sky is up there...

Alice: And the wind... how do you make it?

Giorgia: I make it as does the fan I have at home... it blows hard...

Ilaria: I would like to make a machine which blows flowers as well, as the wind blows flowers as well, it blows also the rain which flies to the sky...

Filippo: Well, if it can blow the flowers, rain, rainbow, it will blow our balloons as well.

The children start drawing; each of them chooses the sheet that best matches the project in his or her mind.

Appendix 2: Giovanni Piazza: The Wind Machine

The project started from a conversation the classroom teachers had with the four-year-old children who had come back from the gym. The children spoke about their activities in the gym and particularly about a game they had played: to direct some balloons, moving them on the floor by blowing, to reach a line marked on the floor.

Among the various remarks, the most interesting appeared to be Simone's: to invent and build a machine able somehow to blow and move balloons in the children's place. Some children joined the proposal. As educators, we teachers discussed the working possibilities of such an idea, taking into account various aspects of the project:

• The group formation. The group was forming around a shared interest in a problem. This was important, even taking into account the children's young age. In fact, all of them had just turned four.

• The level of representation, exchange, and project communication that could arise. Only one girl, Giorgia, in fact used representational shapes, while the rest of the group were in the phase of scribbles.

• The project possibilities of a group of four-year-olds working on an object of big dimensions. The children, in fact, wanted the machine to be "big and strong to produce the wind."

• The children's working capabilities to deal with complex tools.

• The children's abilities to understand a series of structural relations balance, logic, measure, empty and full space relationship, volumes, project circularity.

• Our problems as teachers during the project and building phases. We had no working experience with children of that age. Our only reference points were working experiences with five-year-olds.

After considering all those points, we decided to try to give the children the possibility to test their capacities in this enterprise of theirs; as adults we would be a constant and active presence during the whole process. As teachers, we agreed that our main task was to act as a help to the children's memory in the evolving of the project. We would try to be the children's "containers," to hold their own ideas, words, actions and make them available to them at every moment.

A second help we could offer the children but only when requested by them was to overcome the difficulties implied in the use of the tools that would be necessary to assemble materials.

The group, formed of Giorgia, Simone, Filippo, and Alice, started with the project of the machine which only at a later time was named "The Wind Machine" and then its construction. They met together twenty-two times, for a time varying from forty minutes to two hours each meeting.

The group used instruments such as a camera and a tape-recorder, sheets of paper and graphic and plastic materials to pin down their ideas and solve problems during the process. The possibility of having access to various places the *atelier*, the school laboratory, the classroom *miniatelier* allowed and integrated the forming of different social relations (individual, pair, group). It also gave the children the possibility of immediately turning their insights into action.

The project originated from each child's personal hypotheses, which were then shared, discussed, and negotiated to reach agreement on one single project of the machine. The building of the structure characterized the intermediate phase of the project; it stressed the children's good ability in perceiving three-dimensionality and the importance and difficulty of moving from two-dimensionality their project drawings to three-dimensionality the actual structure. The projects they had drawn were used to realize the machine and monitor (check) the various stages of the work.

In this building phase, the children had to deal with different materials, leading them to confirm or reject the initial project, thus generating the children's researches of different meanings and compromises.

In the last phase of the building, color, paper, iron, and plastic were evocative media in the children's representations in their drawings. The sense of movement absolutely necessary for the children in a wind machine was created by electrical motors such as fans and hair dryers the children brought from home and wanted the teacher to put inside the machine to move balloons set on the "mouth" of the machine.

When the work was completed, the machine was shown to the other children of the class and later to the parents. And this was the end of the children's enterprise.

References

BERNADONI, G. (1988). *Educazione motoria all'immagine, al suono, alla musica*. Bologna, Italy: IRRSEA-ER.

BROUDY, H. (1972). *Enlightened cherishing*. Urbana: University of   Illinois Press. ED 058 244.

DE BARTOLOMEIS, F. (1990). *Il colore dei pensieri e dei sentimenti* [The color of thoughts and feelings]. Firenze, Italy: La Nuova Italia.

DEPARTMENT OF EDUCATION (1987). *I cento linguaggi dei bambini* [The hundred languages of children]. Catalogue of the exhibit of the same name. Reggio Emilia, Italy: Center for Educational Research.

EISNER, E.W. (1985). *The educational imagination*. New York: Macmillan.

ELKIND, D. (1987). *Miseducation: Preschoolers at risk*. New York: Knopf.

GARDNER, H. (1989). *To open minds: Chinese clues to the dilemma of contemporary education*. New York: Basic Books.

GARDNER, H. (1993). Complementary perspectives on Reggio Emilia. In C. Edwards, L. Gandini, and G. Forman (Eds.), *The Hundred Languages of Children: The Reggio Emilia Approach to Early Childhood Education* (pp. ix-xviii). Norwood, NJ: Ablex. ED 355 034.

GOODLAD, J. (1979). *Curriculum inquiry: The study of curriculum practice*. New York: McGraw Hill. ED 181 864.

LODGE, D. (1991). *Small world*. New York: Warner Books.

RABITTI, G. (1992). *Preschool at "La Villetta"*. Master of Arts thesis, University of Illinois at Urbana-Champaign.

STAKE, R.E. (1978). The case study method in social inquiry. *Educational Researcher* 7 (2):5-8.

STAKE R.E., L. BRESLER, and L. MABRY (1991). *Custom and cherishing: The arts in elementary schools*. Urbana: University of Illinois, School of Music.

Promoting Collaborative Learning in the Early Childhood Classroom: Teachers' Contrasting Conceptualizations in Two Communities

Carolyn Edwards
University of Kentucky - Lexington, Kentucky
Lella Gandini
University of Massachusetts-Amherst - Amherst, Massachusetts
John Nimmo
Pacific Oaks College Northwest - Seattle, Washington

Editor's Note: An earlier version of this paper was presented in April 1991 in the symposium "Italian Young Children in Cultural and Learning Contexts" at the annual conference of the American Educational Research Association in Chicago, Illinois. The paper was published under the title Favorire l'apprendimento cooperativo nella prima infanzia: Concettualizzasioni contrastanti degli insegnanti di due comunita *in the journal* Rassegna di Psicologia, *published by the University of Rome, 1992, volume IX(3), pp. 65 90.*

Italy, with its emerging stature as a European leader in quality public child care, has recently become the site of much research by North Americans. Because many American and Italian psychologists share a goal of advancing new ways of understanding socialization and education in context, it is timely to begin to examine and compare methods and findings. When culturally comparative studies are considered, it is of course necessary to remember that national cultures are not unitary: there is no homogeneous "Italian" or "American" culture. Rather, attention to multiplicity, change, and inter- and intra-locale differences are an essential part of the challenge in analyzing the cultural contexts of learning and development at home and school.

Our study should also be considered part of the endeavor in contemporary social science to transform the individualistic assumptions about science, self, and society that have become deeply ingrained in the thinking of North Americans in particular, and of most peoples of the advanced democracies as well. These assumptions have been found to have severe limits for understanding learning and thinking as inherently social processes, for describing socialization as the collective appropriation, rather than internalization, of culture (Bruner, 1986; Rogoff, 1990; Wertsch, 1991), and even, at the most pragmatic level, for working with young children in ways that best promote children's prosocial behavior, empathy, and sense of identification with surrounding reference groups. But just how do we go beyond the individual as the basic unit of analysis in psychology? Theory is slowly being built with key assistance from Vygotskian psychology, cultural anthropology, and interpretive sociolinguistics. At the same time, improved methods of collecting and analyzing data are urgently needed to determine which recommendations will lead in the most fruitful directions.

As evidenced by the articles in the journal *Rassegna di Psicologia*

(1992, volume IX, number 3), psychologists are on the threshold of finding new ways of seeing and then describing learning and socialization as processes of children's participation in communicative events structured by adults.

Statement of the Problem

This particular study was conducted by an intercultural team at three sites: Reggio Emilia (Emilia Romagna, northern Italy), Pistoia (Tuscany, central Italy), and Amherst (Massachusetts, U.S.A.). All three cities share the features of being small, cohesive cities with progressive political traditions and extensive early childhood services. Of the three, however, only Reggio Emilia and Pistoia have built up city-financed, city-managed systems of preprimary and infant-toddler education. Recognized throughout Italy (indeed, Europe) for their quality and innovative substance, these municipal systems are well known as places where professionals and citizens have joined together and put years of effort into creating distinctive public systems that have many noteworthy features, including (1) the ways in which children, teachers, and parents are connected into operative communities focused on the surrounding city and region; and (2) the ways in which children are stimulated toward cognitive, social, and emotional development through collaborative play and group projects.

Such features tend to be quite startling and thought-provoking to the many recent visitors from the United States, who arrive with contrasting perspectives based on North American individualist values and Piagetian assumptions about the egocentrism of young children. Far from causing the American visitors to retreat, however, the process of intercultural confrontation and exchange has proved a strong stimulus for research and discussion.

Our study, in particular, focuses on how teachers in three communi-ties seek to promote collaboration and community in their classrooms. We seek to closely analyze the educators' working philosophies in Reggio Emilia, Pistoia, and Amherst and compare them with their preferred methods of structuring children's schedules, organizing small and large learning groups, managing conflicts, dealing with sex role issues, and connecting children to wider communities outside the classroom. It is an extensive study, and in this paper we report preliminary and partial results only. Even from our preliminary analysis, however, it is evident that each of the three research sites has, as expected, a shared language: what anthropologists (D'Andrade, 1984; Holland & Quinn, 1987; Spradely, 1979) call a "distinctive discourse" or "cultural meaning system," and what psychologist Jerome Bruner (1986) calls a "language of education," for framing issues of collaboration and community regarding young children. This shared language, in turn, can be related to objective practices, that is, methods of school organization and grouping of children, as well as to shared beliefs about the roles of the teacher, the nature of the child as learner, rationales for teacher intervention and guidance, and preferred styles of facilitating the learning process.

In this paper we do not address the larger theoretical problem of how psychologists can best describe learning and thinking as a social process and socialization as the collective appropriation of culture.

Instead, we begin with a question that is empirical indeed, ethnographic: namely, how the different communities of educators in our study talk about teaching and learning as co-action and co-creation of meaning. We will demonstrate that the cultural-community differences are not trivial but rather precisely related to those issues in a way that can be informative to psychologists. It is well known that the thinking of most developmental theorists, especially those influenced by the philosophical foundations of Western Europe and North America, is packaged in individualistic categories (Sampson, 1988; Schwartz, 1990; Triandis, 1989; Triandis et al., 1990). In contrast, our Italian informants, especially those from Reggio Emilia, have developed different philosophical categories not only in their minds as sets of beliefs and values, but also in practice, embodied in coherent institutions and functioning routines. These categories, we will demonstrate, posit learning as co-creation of knowledge and posit the child as inherently social. The Reggio Emilia educators have, over the past thirty years, collectively developed a language of education that assumes a co-constructionist view of the child and of teaching and learning that is very close to that proposed by Jerome Bruner (1986) in *Actual Minds, Possible Worlds*, as illustrated in this quotation:

I have come increasingly to recognize that most learning in most settings is a communal activity, a sharing of the culture. It is not just that the child must make his knowledge his own, but that he must make it his own in a community of those who share his sense of belonging to a culture. It is this that leads me to emphasize not only discovery and invention but the importance of negotiating and sharing in a word, of joint culture creating as an object of schooling and as an appropriate step en route to becoming a member of the adult society in which one lives out one's life. (p. 127)

Rather than focusing on the developing child as an autonomous learner, Reggio Emilia and Pistoia educators see education as a communal activity and sharing of culture through collaboration among children and also between children and teachers, who open topics to speculation and negotiation (see Bruner, 1986, chapter 9). The Amherst, Massachusetts, educators, in contrast, see education first and foremost as a means for promoting the development of each individual. At the same time, however, as will be shown, although their discourse is guided by Western individualistic categories, it is not exhaustively constrained by those terms. Rather, as they grapple on the theoretical level with issues of collaboration and community, and as they engage on the practical level with an actual classroom of children with its own identity and ongoing history, they too respond to the dialectic between the needs of the individual and those of the group. For all of the teachers in our study, then, we believe that their words, framed within images of everyday practice and decision making, reveal a complex picture of the meaning of collaborative learning. The interviews and discussions in the study communities provide us with alternative models of thinking about how collaboration corresponds to an image of the child, an image of the role of the teacher, and a preferred approach to structuring children's experiences. This paper will illustrate the data and point to the emerging findings by comparing some of the views on collaborative learning of the Reggio Emilia and Amherst educators.

Method

Description of Amherst and Reggio Emilia

Reggio Emilia, a city of about 130,000 people, is located in the Emilia Romagna region. In Reggio Emilia, the municipal early childhood program originated in cooperative schools started by parents at the end of World War II. The city currently supports twenty-two preprimary schools for children three to six years of age, as well as thirteen infant-toddler centers for children under three (Edwards et al., 1993). Children of all socioeconomic and educational backgrounds attend the programs, including special needs children; fifty percent of the city's three- to six-year-olds and thirty-seven percent of the city's children who are under three years of age are served in the municipal schools and centers.

Amherst is a town of about 35,000 people in rural western Massachusetts. Founded in 1755, it is known throughout the United States for its many fine universities and colleges located nearby, as well as for its historic town-meeting form of democratic governance and citizen participation and its long tradition of political progressivism, manifested in abolitionist efforts during the slavery era and antiwar activities during the Vietnam conflict. In terms of early childhood education, nevertheless, Amherst, while very liberal by American standards, has no unified municipal public child care system. Rather, the town is the site of multiple but piecemeal services: a town-financed central office of information and referral; one town-subsidized infant-toddler center that serves town employees' children; numerous high-quality preschools in the private domain; a network of licensed day care homes supervised by the state of Massachusetts; programs or slots for handicapped, disadvantaged, or abused preschool-aged children, financed by the city or the state; and free universal kindergarten education classrooms to serve all five-and six-year-olds as the first year of public primary education (Edwards & Gandini, 1989; Nimmo, 1992).

Interview Methods

Our methodology in all three sites involved a combination of teacher interviews with an adaptation of the "multi-vocal video-ethnography" developed by Tobin, Wu, and Davidson (1989) and described in their book, *Preschool in Three Cultures*. In this method, videotapes of classroom activity are obtained not to document and represent the classrooms, but rather as a stimulus and starting point for a critical and reflective dialogue with the ultimate goal of constructing a *multi-vocal video-ethnography* (Tobin, 1988; Tobin et al., 1989).

Researchers systematically elicit (and record) the reactions to videotaped classroom segments of a series of cultural insiders and outsiders: the focal teachers, colleagues at their school, parents, educators and parents from other cities in their own country, and finally educators and parents from other countries. These reactions are assembled, analyzed, and interpreted by the ethnographer, who thereby takes responsibility for the final product, in a report that seeks to preserve the multiplicity of the perspectives or voices of all the people involved.

First, we selected a small group of teachers in each city to be our central informants. We wanted these teachers to be members of an educational community, that is, a coherent group of educators who possessed a shared professional language and set of core values concerning teaching. At the same time, we desired to work with informants who were considered, by their own peers and administrators, to be strong exemplars of their craft and articulate spokespersons for their values and practices. In each city, therefore, we consulted extensively with school administrators, who thereby became deeply involved in the study and indeed made good use of it for their own purposes (incorporating our research in their ongoing inservice staff development endeavors). In Reggio Emilia, where the entire municipal early childhood education system constitutes an educational community, we were directed by the central administration to work with the teachers of one preprimary school, the Scuola Diana, where the *atelierista* was the most experienced in the system and which was favored by a stable teaching staff and outstanding physical environment. In this school, which contained the standard three classrooms for three-, four-, and five-year-olds, we had done extensive slide photography and videotaping in 1988 and therefore had already established good rapport. In Amherst, in contrast, where there was no unified public early childhood system, in order to obtain a group of teachers who belonged to a self-conscious educational community, we interviewed teachers at the Common School, a highly regarded, progressive, independent school serving children ages three to twelve, with three mixed-age classrooms for preprimary children (two classrooms for three- and four-year-olds and one classroom for five- and six-year-olds) and four mixed-age primary classes.

The first stage of data gathering was *initial interviewing* to learn about the teachers' concepts of collaboration and community building. Teachers were given the questions earlier so that they could think about or talk over their answers if they wished. We asked a standard set of open-ended questions, as follows:
• Do you see learning in the age group you work with as a collaborative process? Why or why not? Can you give some examples from your classroom experience?
• How do you as a teacher foster children learning from other children in your classroom? What problems or blocks have you encountered?
• Do you see children in your age group adopting shared goals in free or structured play? Can you give some examples?
• Do you see children commenting on or responding to each other's work? How do you respond to this kind of interaction? Is it something you want to encourage or influence in any way?
• Do you see your classroom as a community? If so, in what way?

• How do you connect your children to wider communities? Can you give some examples?
• What are the limitations to the kind of community you can create with your age group of children?
• How about cross-sex relations? What are the limitations to the community and collaboration that can occur between the sexes?

The second, and most extensive, stage of data gathering involved videotaping in the teachers' classrooms during morning activity time on two occasions and then using the videotapes in a playback session called the *video-reflective interview*; this discussion with the teachers was also videotaped. The initial classroom videotapes were collected in Reggio by the teacher participants working with their art director (*atelierista*), but in the other two cities by the research team. The research team then worked together to select a series of segments for video playback, trying to include episodes representative of different kinds of social activity (teacher-child, child-child, conflictual, and cooperative). (In doing this selection, we used information gathered in the prior interviews to be sure to include the kinds of events considered important for collaboration and community building by the relevant teachers, as well as episodes we thought interesting or significant, from our own perspectives.) We also worked together to generate one or more questions to ask regarding each segment, always beginning with an open-ended request, "Tell us about this segment, in terms of the social issues involved," and followed by a specific probe, such as, "Can you comment on this episode in terms of cross-sex relations?" The subsequent video-reflective interviews lasted two to three hours each and took place in a small group that consisted of the teacher (or co-teachers) of the pertinent classroom, sometimes other teachers from their school, sometimes one or more administrators from their system, and two or more members of the research team. They were videotaped for later analysis and later transcribed in full.

In the third and final stage of data gathering, we engaged the educators in *cross-cultural video-reflective discussions*. Gathering together all of the study participants from the city, plus many of their colleagues from other preschools interested in the research, we showed segments from the other research site and asked people to comment on what they saw that was congruent with and discrepant from their professional values, as well as what they saw that was similar and dissimilar to their own classrooms. These discussions, conducted in Reggio and Pistoia concerning Amherst, and in Amherst concerning both Italian sites, were extremely useful in revealing the most deeply held beliefs and values of the different participants, as well as some value-oriented reactions to the other system's practices.

Thus the videotape segments were never intended to capture the objective reality of the classroom: obviously, the segments were not representative in any sampling sense; and furthermore, videotape, with its complex juxtaposition of images and words, has to be interpreted to gain meaning. The meaning necessarily shifts, depending on who is looking and what they are thinking about as they look. Instead, we used video playback in a way similar to, but extending beyond, the format known as *stimulated recall* (a qualitative technique used in research on teaching to investigate individual teachers' interactive thoughts and decision making (Calderhead, 1981; Tuckwell, 1980). That is, by having the video-reflective interview take place in a group setting, we stimulated people to talk and listen to one another, to agree and disagree, and to modify their ideas as the discussion proceeded, and thus to co-construct their descriptions, interpretations, and analyses.

Preliminary Findings

The richness of our data exceeded our expectations and testifies to the strength of the video-reflection methodology as well as the articulateness and thoughtfulness of our informants. We are performing a formal textual analysis of the interview and discussion materials, looking at expressed concepts surrounding issues of collaboration and community understood in their broadest senses. This analysis is guided by the foundational assumption that qualitative analysis should begin as soon as data are collected and continue to emerge throughout the entire project in order to construct "grounded theory" (Glaser & Strauss, 1967; Lincoln & Guba, 1985; Nimmo, 1992). In contrast to *a priori* theory, grounded theory is more responsive to, and able to encompass, the contextual elements and multiple realities encountered in this type of qualitative research. Accordingly, therefore, the research team has developed a set of coding categories that refer to all the key words and central themes appearing in the corpus of interviews and discussions and relate to ideas concerning collaboration, cooperation, community, co-action, social exchange and connection, communication, and other related concepts (as well as their contrasts: conflicts, miscommunications, individualistic acts and values, disunities, social segregation, and so forth). The resulting set of approximately one hundred categories has been used to code all interviews and discussions, using a qualitative text analysis program, The Ethnograph (Seidel et al., 1988), which allows segments of text to be assigned multiple codings for later selective retrieval and interpretation. The findings of the study will emerge from the processes of interpretation and comparison.

In this paper, we will provide a preliminary "reading" of the data by demonstrating how distinct the contrast is between ways of approaching young children's classroom collaboration in Reggio Emilia and Amherst. In a future monograph, we will analyze all of the major concepts and themes for the three study communities: Amherst, Pistoia, and Reggio Emilia. Here, we will simply illustrate the directions that analysis will take by showing how different were two of the communities of educators, as revealed in one component of the data: their answers on the initial collaboration interview, in particular, their responses to question one ("Do you see learning in the age group you work with as a collaborative process? Why or why not? Can you give some examples from your classroom experience?"). Almost any segments of the material would have served for these present purposes; however, we have selected for comparison answers to the first question in the interview because they arose from the initial moments of the data-gathering encounter between the teachers and ourselves, and, as such, carry a particularly potent charge in terms of communication of meaning. We consider that these answers offer useful entry points to the systems of meaning that the teachers were seeking to convey to us. Furthermore, by selecting for close analysis the answers to a single question, we are able to reveal the precise differences in the discourse used by the two communities of teachers and begin to understand the similarities and differences in outlook and issues of concern for the two groups of educators. We found that the statements made about collaboration and community in the initial interviews were then clarified, indeed, "acted out" through the social processes of the group discussions in the video-reflective interviews. The cross-cultural video-reflective discussions, finally, brought some closure to the data gathering and revealed core issues of concern to each group within itself as well as a sense of what aspects of the other community's approach were most similar and dissimilar to its own preferred ways.

The Collaboration Interview: Opening Statements
of the Reggio Emilia Educators

One of the more senior teachers in the Diana School, PS, made a concise opening statement that put forward several premises we were to hear over and over in Reggio Emilia: the importance of collaboration (she calls it "co-action") to intellectual development; the need for moments of conflict as well as moments of cooperation; the unity of cognitive and affective development; the importance of the physical environment for making collaboration among children possible; and the collaborative model provided by the teachers' collective. When she used the phrase, "Here in Reggio we are convinced . . . ," she made clear her sense of identification with the ongoing educational experience in Reggio Emilia. She re-emphasized this same idea at the end of her opening statement, describing her own professional formation and sense of affinity with the methods of work in her system.

PS: I do think that the children each child gets an advantage by staying with other children. Here in Reggio we are convinced that the cognitive learning and the affective development are tied to co-action of children and also to conflict. We are part of a project that is based on co-action of children and on the sureness that this is a good way of learning. Therefore, I find this question justified, and I see that there is learning as a collaborative process.
I can give examples. One concerns the Oil Project that we did with children. And we should also look at the physical environment [of the school] where children can stay in small groups, and where the teachers, who already cooperate among themselves, form what we call a collective. The teachers cooperate.
Actually, I am a special case [as a teacher] because I studied to be an elementary teacher. . . . I must say, I did not have much experience with young children in fact, none; but I immediately became completely fascinated by the different way the schools are run here. . . . From then on, I have been completely taken, and I have decided that this way of working is very congenial to me.

A second senior teacher, LR, opened her reply with a parallel declaration of belief in the validity and correctness of the Reggio Emilia method of working with small groups of children on long-term projects. She then went on to say many significant things about the use of small groups. She noted that small groups allow the teacher to readily enter the children's world and embark with them on an intellectual journey. She defined what this journey is about: asking questions and seeking knowledge. She referred to the working partnership of the fundamental Reggio triangle, teachers-children-parents, in noting how children draw their parents into their inquiries, and then the parents go to the teachers with questions. She then briefly reflected upon the fact that young children actively form their own peer relationships; through observation she has learned how important are these spontaneous groups to the process of children's becoming able to understand (communicate with) one another. Finally, she provided a long example of her project work with small groups of children and explained much about the teacher's role in Reggio, facilitating children's communication by listening for fruitful ideas, acting as the group "memory," and helping children represent their ideas in symbolic form. Here is what LR said to the opening question about fostering collaboration among young children.

LR: It is a way of working not only valid but also right. I, as a teacher, succeed in reading much more and in understanding, in staying within the group as an adult. There is much interest even from me. It is a relationship between me and the children: my staying with them becomes a way to help them to face a problem. I grow up with the children. I work in a state of uncertainty because I do not know where the children can arrive to, but it is a fabulous experience. . . .
In the last two years we have assisted the kids who set problems within the group; they ask other children or adults about complex problems. The *whys* they ask are very important and lead to the discovery of being able to solve problems. Kids are always in contact with the work they do; they always ask, "Why?" They inform themselves; they find that what they say and what they do are considered by the adult; they find adults who collaborate with them, for example, their family. Parents are interested in the work children do and come to us with questions.
Last year we had very young children; they had just entered the preschool. We have always observed them, and we noticed that they were inclined to form groups. The children picked out those kids with whom they have lasting relationships. Our work as adults is based also on the observation of these groups, because their staying together in groups permits them to discover one another. Perhaps if they didn't form groups, it would take them longer to understand the others.
[Can you give an example of fostering collaboration?]
Last year, each of the two teachers had to carry on a project which would be brought to an end. We had to be present and absent. We had to catch the right moments to intervene. Kids greatly appreciated the fact of hearing, saying, intervening; and this makes their interest grow within the group, especially in young kids. I had to gather together all the points touched on and remember them. "Where shall we arrive?" I

used to ask myself. Children discovered the adult and used her. They used her and her means. "Tell us what we said!" They give, but they want you to give as well. They want to receive.

I then refused to be their memory and proposed a visible form of memory, so we (or better, they) had to translate their ideas into a language comprehensible to them all. The possibilities were many: graphics, simulations, etc.

Since that time, we have always been asking them to do that at once, to give them the opportunity to explain themselves in a better way. And this requires making oneself understood by the others, which is a strong motivation. Other kids often intervene. This is useful as they help the other child to explain himself and to make clear his ideas. For example, when studying colored shadows, kids had transparent, colored books. These books made a colored shadow not a black shadow, as people and animals do. They had to explain this: "Why don't the books make a black shadow?" The experience was really very good.

The younger member of LR's co-teaching team, MC, was interviewed later. Rather than make abstract statements about the place of collaborative learning in the Reggio Emilia pedagogy, she simply sought to describe what the process of collaborative learning looks like, using the example of a videotaped session involving herself and two boys. She described how the children confronted their shared problem, formed a bond, generated a "fan" of ideas, sought each other's opinions and suggestions, and persevered until (rather surprisingly) they achieved the solution of a very difficult problem. She added that this kind of collaborative problem solving is less likely to appear when children are in their entire class of twenty-five.

MC: Certainly the possibilities that a child encounters inside a school are varied and diversified; cooperation understood as a `system of relations' not only on the personal level, but in learning to be together with others, facing things together is an important part because it can increase the qualitative level of one's ideas as compared to others, such as we've observed in the video [in which I work with two boys who are seeking to draw a picture with a computer-activated Logo turtle]. Those two children faced a problem, in which it clearly showed them the meaning of solving together, of how one plus its counterpart confronted the problem and proved how this bond clearly was established, this "fan" of ideas and support to help one think and build on ideas, with the support of others. It was actually something of a surprise the way they solved the problem. There is an element of surprise every time one sees and observes such a bond being formed among the children. Their independent decision, "swing of ideas" (exchange), hesitation, and gradual formation of a unified decision, finally turns toward the "house." One is truly amazed, for one could not have suspected such an outcome at the beginning of the episode.

This type of observation we can make not only as in this instance with the two children, but also in all instances of learning, cooperation, and in all contexts. A group of twenty-five children as a unified body may or may not show us this elaborate process of cooperation with one another, such as we may see in smaller groups, such as a group of four children, six, or eight, where the number determines what can be accomplished in respect to cooperation. As in our previous example, with the two children on video, these were children who knew one another and experienced together this new situation in which one could see the diverging thoughts and varied processes, but also the seeking of each other's opinions and suggestions. Though diverging at first, they did not drop their common project but instead arrived at a final decision together.

Finally, in a joint interview with a co-teaching pair, MB and MM, the initial statement addressed issues also frequently raised by the others in later parts of their interviews or in the group discussions, namely, what factors age, sex, prior experience, group size and composition influ-ence young children's capacities to collaborate in problem solving. MB and MM noted that for the youngest children (three-years-old), prior friendships formed in the nido (infant-toddler center) are the starting point for collaboration in the preprimary school. Moreover, the collaborative process in three-year-olds looks different, more simple based on comparison, exchange, and proximity than among older children. Finally, they referred to two issues then a focus of attention among the Reggio system as a whole: what size of group (two, three, four, five, or more children) works best in project work?; and how do sex differences affect social process and style of problem solving?

MB and MM: In our class there are twenty-five children, three-year-olds, and twenty-three of those twenty-five are coming from the nido. In fact, ten are coming from one nido. We start with fact that because it is a very important element in cooperation. Of course, three-year-olds are very different from four- and five-year-olds, but even at the nido level, especially the last year, they start making friends. So some of the children who come in [to the preprimary school] at three already have their favorite friends. They arrive in groups that are already quite settled. In fact, for them it is almost more important to be together than to have the same teacher. So this part is very important.
Indeed, the collaborative process is very much in operation at this age. It's very important. It's very what one does, generally, is close to another child. So although there is not always an exchange, just to be near another person is a very important element.
One should never separate the cognitive and social aspects, speaking of a child, because a child is a whole and when the child learns, he learns as a whole. And it's very important to have a friend nearby when one learns so one can compare, just compare what one learns in a very approximate way. The best relationship at this age is between two children a couple that forms spontaneously. One child looks for one other child, not for two or three other children. And at three, the couples can be of the same sex or of different sex. They don't seem to be so aware, or to have problems in playing with children of the opposite sex at this age. But when children become four or five this [sex difference] makes a big difference. And also one thing that is important to keep in

mind is that although the children are three years old, actually there is a big range because of the birthdays, some could have the birthday in December or January, so it's quite a wide age range.

In sum, in their opening remarks, the Reggio Emilia educators introduced key aspects of how they view collaboration. Not only what they said was significant, but equally what they did not say. They stressed their identification with the collective nature of their work, and did not differentiate their individual thoughts from those of the larger reference group. Conflict was mentioned as a part of productive communication, rather than as a negative to be avoided, and they did not state any limits to the amount of group work children should do. They noted the importance of small group size in allowing fruitful exchange and dialogue, and did not describe the group as coercive over the individual. They defined the teacher's role in facilitating communication, and did not state any general ways teachers tend to, or should try to, restrain the development of collaborations or cliques between children. Finally, they spoke of the need to observe spontaneous social processes the natural formation of friendships, the approach-avoidance relations of boys and girls as a part of understanding children's social possibilities, and they did not volunteer these factors, or developmental or personality factors, as intractable obstacles to any child's participation in collaborative project work. The Amherst teachers, as we shall see, were much more conservative about what they saw as dangers or limitations to collaboration in young children.

The Collaboration Interview: Opening Statements
of the Amherst Educators

The teachers in the Common School worked in teaching teams, with each classroom having a head teacher supervising one or two assistant teachers. All of the classrooms are mixed-age, containing the equivalent of two age-grades. This organization is intended to give each child alternating experiences of being one of the older and one of the younger members in the classroom group; to increase the amount of inter-child helping; to reduce competition and invidious comparisons of children's abilities; and to support teachers in giving children one-to-one attention.

One of these head teachers, GS, who worked in one of the three- and four-year-old classrooms, began by affirming that collaboration, in the "social sense," is critical to the mission of early education.

In her view, the shared setting of preschool requires that children negotiate how to "get along with each other." Children contribute individual input into this process through problem-solving discussions. However, GS stressed that she and her teaching team do not generally plan for shared projects within the curriculum. Individual ownership of products remains of primary value for both children and teachers. In part, these individual products stand as a representation of each child's activity and even his or her identity.

GS: Well there would be no need to have children to come to school if it weren't that they need to cooper.... ah... collaborate with each other. You know the whole purpose of a nursery school is that the children have interactions with other children and therefore have to learn how to get along with other people. In the social sense we totally collaborate all the time. You know, "Who can do what?" and "Who can be where?" and "What is alright to play with who?" and how to be with other people. I mean, everything the whole time has to do with working with other people.

When it comes to actual set-up by teachers, organized work, we do relatively little that is a project that all of them work on at the same time. We might put a project together after each one individually worked on their part. We might then put it together, either as a display together, or we stick it together and make something out of it or, you know, use it in that way, but, when. . . in the whole art area most of the time each child works on their own project and takes it home . . . eventually.

There is quite a lot of emphasis on bringing a project home: to some extent because you are part of your project, but another extent to communicate with the parents what the children are doing at school. My reason for putting stuff in a bag in the drawer [for parents to pick up and take home], even though the kid might have lost interest at that point, is that it's an easy way to tell the parent that he's been painting today. . . you know, so it's nice to let them see it even if they just toss it out. On the other hand, the kids often get attached to what they do and often want to take stuff home. So, there is a lot of emphasis on your own thing, what you make.

But when it comes to getting along with other people and working together and... so we do a lot of problem solving together. We will have, for instance, on Friday we had a discussion on "What can we do so we don't make the play-house so messy that we're not able to clean it up anymore?" and then we let the children speak on that subject matter and we try to use their suggestions, if there are any we can agree on. So we talked about it and what we came to on Friday was that we will only have four children there for a little while and see if that makes it better. It's not a finished discussion of the problem, there will be discussion of this for the next six weeks [laughs]... that happened last year too...!

The opening statement of MS, head teacher of the other three- and four-year-old classroom, also immediately raised the inevitability of collaboration arising within a shared setting. That MS sees this collaboration as involving the "incorporation of each other's ideas," hints at the Amherst school's attention to perspective taking as a vehicle for both intellectual and social development. While acknowledging her focus on the "individual" (note that she uses the word, "individual," seven times in her first three sentences), MS argued that encouraging children's autonomous action actually makes collaboration possible; that is, through shared knowledge of each peer's contribution of individuality to the "unique group." Finally, MS asserts the much repeated view of the Amherst educators, that collaboration best occurs "naturally" within child-initiated activity" rather than in projects directed by teachers.

MS: I see it [learning] as a collaborative process in the sense that there are twenty individuals in the classroom sharing in activities and social interchange with each other, and within that setting we're bound to collaborate and share with and incorporate each other's ideas. I think we tend to focus more on individual projects and individual strengths of the kids and encourage their self-initiative and confidence in themselves. And in the process, I think that draws our attention to those individual traits attention to each child as an individual but in that sense we make up a unique group, with each individual within the group. The kids collaborating together comes out of their knowledge and understanding of each other as individuals.

[Can you give examples?]

There are lots of little groups that gather. For instance, today there was a group playing with Playmobile, with pirates and boats, and collaborating on a shared fantasy theme. We have a marker [pens] area that's pretty much independent where teachers and kids go off and draw together. I've heard kids discussing, "Oh, you make a really nice house. Houses are hard for me, but I can do this well." Kids showing, "Well, I do a house this way," and sort of sharing their different strategies for drawing. At the water tables with different kinds of pumps, I've seen one kid pumping water and another kid putting a trough underneath and cooperating to catch the water and direct the water in different directions. It tends in our classroom to be child-initiated types of collaboration more than teacher-facilitated, although we do make a conscious effort to set up situations where that can happen naturally kids collaborating on projects. If we're setting up a corn starch goop activity with different colors and bowls, we'd do it at a round table where kids would have the opportunity to pass and share the colors and mix them, saying, "Can I have some of your green and I'll put in some of my yellow."

Similar to her colleagues, BJ, the head teacher in the five- and six-year-old classroom, held that collaboration is grounded in children having opportunities to contribute their ideas to the group's curriculum. Children take ownership of the curriculum through having this "voice in it." BJ believes that this sense of participation presents the best potential for collaborative effort between children. As a teacher she aims to act as a facilitator. From BJ's perspective, the autonomy she encourages offers the children considerable freedom to truly negotiate ideas with peers. This process involves the (worthwhile) risk of giving over some teacher control of the curriculum. Here is her opening statement:

BJ: I like to give space to the children to interact with the curriculum. . . to get their ideas into what we are learning and in that sense I see it as a collaborative effort. Whatever we are studying, the children should have a voice in it in a way that they can feel that they can express their own ideas and influence the way that curriculum goes. It becomes a very variable thing, uneven some days and some times you feel the need to take charge of what's going on and give it direction, and other times there are many opportunities where you can just go with the flow, with what the children are suggesting to you.

[Can you give examples?]
I guess, as an example: one of the things I love to do is plays, and we did a play this fall that involved insects, because we were studying them and the children made up the play and decided what part they would play in it. The children are not at the point where they work wonderfully well at accepting each other's ideas, but they were able to sustain what came out of the group as a whole, and I helped them put it together. But it was their ideas, and they bought into it, and they worked together and did a slightly crazy. . . but it was their ideas and it was childlike in its conception and fun and successful. My own experience has been that feeding kids lines in a play is never half as successful, particularly with young children, as saying, "Who would you like to be in this play?" And people know what they want to be and what they can be doing and [in that way] build the play from the ground up.

The final opening statement comes from RA, presently the head teacher of the six- to eight-year-old classroom but for many years the head teacher of three- and four-year-olds. She distinguished between projects that foster collaboration and those that do not. Yet, even when children are focused on "personal goals," RA still identifies collaboration as happening in the "give and take" of individual perspectives that occurs in a group setting. This process is reminiscent of the "incorporation of ideas" noted by MS earlier. As teacher, RA supports this exchange through modeling. With these older children, though, RA also plans curricula that will necessitate children coming together collaboratively in pursuit of "common goals," such as when making a large group sculpture. She also describes clearly the way in which the organizational feature of a mixed-age group plays a key role in promoting inter-child nurturance and cooperation. Even when talking about these activities, however, RA still emphasizes the individual when she discusses the process of peer "consultation" in collaborative projects and the way mixed-age grouping allows teachers to provide children with "individual attention."

RA: I think it depends on what they are doing. There are certain things we plan with collaboration in mind. For instance, this past semester we studied the culture of Indians, and there were certain things the children worked on on their own and were their [individual] projects. However, even in those situations they worked at tables in groups, and there's a lot of give and take. There's a lot going back and forth, and the teachers will model a lot of this. Because very often a teacher will be doing a similar sort of project and might lean over and say [to a child], "Oh, how did you get that to do that over there?" and modeling that kind of questioning and answering, so the children will do it with each other. But, the end result is something they own themselves and take away with them, and that tends to be something that happens a lot.
And so what we try to do is think of things that necessitate them all working toward a common goal as opposed to working toward a personal goal. One of the parents came in who works a lot with clay and they built a huge clay horse modeled on Indian terra-cotta sculpture. And they all knew that [it] was something that no one was going to take

away with them, and they all had to work on it together. And there was a lot more consultation, "Oh, what do you think would look good here? How should we make the legs?" So there was a lot more collaboration that went on with something like that. So I think that learning can be [collaborative], depending on the task.

[Is this a mixed-age group you are working with?]

Yes, there are six-, seven-, and eight-year-olds. So that also changes the dynamics, because the older children know the ropes and are very often called upon to help the new fledglings coming in and show them what to do and how to do it. I think the older children tend to be more collaborative. They seem to feel like they know what is going on, and it's their role it's built into the operation of the classroom that in order to provide the individual attention that we like to give children, they need to assume a role in which they are helping [younger children].

Together, the Common School teachers introduced key aspects of how they view collaboration. Their use of "we," speaking of the teachers' perspective, was reminiscent of the Reggio educators and reflected the strong sense of collegial partnership within each of the teaching teams and within the school as a whole. In defining collaboration, they talked about the impact of the shared ecology of the classroom and the mixed-age grouping that promote spontaneous collaboration through play, mutual helping, and exchange of ideas. They made a distinction that we never heard in Reggio Emilia: between this kind of child-initiated collaboration, rooted in spontaneous social interaction, and a kind that is teacher-initiated, taking place in the context of group problem-solving discussions or teacher-initiated projects like doing a play or building a large sculpture. Teachers preferred the spontaneous, child-initiated collaborations and the group problem-solving discussions as the most valuable and appropriate experiences for young, preprimary children.

It is interesting that, in spite of coming squarely out of the politically and pedagogically leftist Progressive Education tradition, these teachers followed the common American habit of using many words and phrases that originated from the domain of property relations and transactions: BJ says that children "bought into" the play idea; RA talks about children doing work they "own themselves" and offering ideas in "consultation."

They talked on several occasions about "investment" and "input" into the curriculum "owned" by all. This can be seen as complementary to their Deweyian vision of the school as a democratic community in which each individual has an equal voice and active participation. In general, their emphasis is on children's individual self-development and how this can be enhanced through friendship, mutual helping, play, perspective taking, group problem solving, and as children grow older, genuine collaborative project work. These issues (and others) emerged repeatedly in subsequent interviews in the data gathering: in the dialogues held with each teaching team; and the two large meetings for cross-cultural video-reflection.

Conclusion

Beginning with shared assumptions about the nature of the child and of schooling as a "system of relations and communications embedded in the wider social system" (Rinaldi, 1990), the educators in Reggio Emilia have developed over the past thirty years a distinctive approach to early education. The concrete features of this approach include, as key components, small group collaborative learning; continuity over time of child-child and child-teacher relations; a focus on problem solving and long-term projects involving mastery of many symbolic media; fostering of the connections between home, school, and the wider community; and awareness and appreciation of cultural heritage (city, region, and nation). Accompanying these concrete organizational features is a shared discourse or language of education that allows the Reggio teachers to collaborate, that is, in their own terms, to exchange ideas, listen to one another, and engage in meaningful conflict over ideas. Their language of education is readily apparent in their statements in the collaboration interviews, as well as the subsequent group video-reflection discussions. It is based on a theory of knowledge that defines thinking and learning as social and communicative events co-constructive experiences for both children and adults.

The Amherst educators, members of a school community founded in the 1960s and based on Deweyian principles of progressive education, likewise have developed a shared language of education. Central to their goals are promoting the development of each unique individual, within a strong community stretching backward and forward in time and containing children, their families, and all the staff at the school director, librarian, teachers, assistant teachers, and others. This community is conceived as democratic, diverse, and drawing strength from the ties of cross-age relationships. Their language of education, very different from that heard in Reggio Emilia, is based on a theory of knowledge that sees thinking and learning as a matter of each child gaining knowledge of self, others, and the wider world through social interaction, research, and discussion processes that stimulate the development of mature autonomy and self-realization. Placing the two perspectives in juxtaposition, it is easy to see how each language of education constrains or directs the thinking of its teachers, but at the same time packages ideas economically to make communication and dialogue possible for the community. The language of education preferred in Amherst focuses teachers' attention on individuals and how they develop and change over time. The preferred discourse makes it difficult for them to regard groups as the always desirable context for intellectual work and supports the view that teachers should closely monitor social interactions between children and be available to work closely in short, one-on-one or one-on-two spurts, with children engaged in intellectual work, so that children have opportunities for both guided and independent learning. In contrast, the language of education preferred in Reggio Emilia focuses teachers' attention on children always in relation to the group, and makes it difficult for them to speak systematically about the value of their program in terms of what the children gain from it, year by year, across specific domains.

At the same time, the educators in each community seem to be aware of more dimensions and more complexity than what their language of education structures for them. As we shall discuss in future writings, both groups of teachers are highly aware of the unique personality of each child and also highly knowledgeable about the group processes in their classroom. Indeed, it appeared that the interviews and discussions involved in our research, particularly the cross-cultural video-reflection, provoked the teachers to consider the limitations of both their own and the other community's discourse and practices.

References

BRUNER, J. (1986). Actual minds, possible worlds. Cambridge, MA: Harvard University Press.

CALDERHEAD, J. (1981). Stimulated recall: A method for research on teaching. British Journal of Educational Psychology 51(2, Jun):211- 217. EJ 251 802.

D'ANDRADE, R.G. (1984). Cultural meaning systems. In R.A. Shweder and R.A. LeVine (Eds.), Culture theory: Essays on mind, self, and emotion (pp. 88-118). New York: Cambridge University Press.

EDWARDS, C., L. GANDINI, and G. FORMAN. (Eds.). (1993). The hundred languages of children: The Reggio Emilia approach to early childhood education. Norwood, NJ: Ablex. ED 355 034.

EDWARDS, C.P., and L. GANDINI. (1989). Teachers' expectations about the timing of developmental skills: A cross-cultural study. Young Children 44(4, May):15-19. EJ 391 009.

GLASER, B.G., and A.L. STRAUSS. (1967). The discovery of grounded theory: Strategies for qualitative research. Chicago: Aldine.

HOLLAND, D., and N. QUINN. (Eds.). (1987). Cultural models in language and thought. New York: Cambridge University Press.

LINCOLN, Y.S., and E. G. GUBA. (1985). Naturalistic inquiry. Beverly Hills, CA: Sage.

NIMMO, J.W. (1992). Classroom community: Its meaning as negotiated by teachers of young children. Unpublished doctoral dissertation, School of Education, University of Massachusetts, Amherst.

RINALDI, C. (1990). Social constructivism in Reggio Emilia, Italy. Paper presented at the annual conference of the Association of Constructivist Teachers, Northampton, Massachusetts, October. Translated into English by B. Rankin, L. Gandini, and K. Ellis.

ROGOFF, B. (1990). Apprenticeship in thinking. New York: Oxford University Press.

SAMPSON, E.E. (1988). The debate on individualism: Indigenous psychologies of the individual and their role in personal and societal functioning. American Psychologist 4(1):15-22.

SCHWARTZ, S.H. (1990). Individualism-collectivism: Critique and proposed refinements. Journal of Cross-Cultural Psychology 21(2, Jun):139-157. EJ 411 278.

SEIDEL, J.V., R. Kjolseth, and E. Seymour. (1988). The ethnograph: A user's guide (version 3.0). Littleton, CO: Qualis Research Associates.

SPRADLEY, J.P. (1979). The ethnographic interview. New York: Holt, Rinehart, and Winston.

TOBIN, J.J. (1988). Visual anthropology and multivocal ethnography: A dialogical approach to Japanese preschool class size. Dialectical Anthropology, 13(2):173-187.

TOBIN, J.J., D.Y.H. WU, and D.H. Davidson. (1989). Preschool in three cultures: Japan, China, and the United States. New Haven, CT: Yale University Press.

TRIANDIS, H.C. (1989). Cross-cultural studies of individualism and collectivism. In J. Berman (Ed.), Nebraska Symposium on Motivation, 1989

(p. 41-133). Lincoln, NE: University of Nebraska Press.

TRIANDIS, H.C., C. McCUSKER, and C.H. HUI. (1990). Multimethod probes of individualism and collectivism. Journal of Personality and Social Psychology 59(5):1006-1020.

TUCKWELL, N.B. (1980). Stimulated recall: Theoretical perspectives and practical and technical considerations. Center for Research in Teaching, University of Alberta, Occasional Paper Series, Technical Report 8-2-3.

WERTSCH, J.V. (1991). Voices of the mind: A sociocultural approach to mediated action. Cambridge, MA: Harvard University Press.

Selected ERIC Bibliography on Reggio Emilia and the Reggio Emilia Approach

Items in this bibliography were selected from a search of the ERIC database. Items published or entered into the database between September 1990 and October 1994 are included in the bibliography. ERIC documents and journal articles are listed in descending order, from most recently added to the database to least recently added to the database.

ERIC Documents

ED369519 PS022240
Educare in Europe. Report of the European Child Care Conference
(Copenhagen, Denmark, October 1992).
United Nations Educational, Scientific, and Cultural Organization,
Paris (France).
[1994; 152p.
ISBN: 87-7738-027-4
Available From: The Young Child and the Family Environment Project, UNESCO, 7, Place de Fontenoy, 75352 Paris 07 SP, France.
EDRS Price - MF01/PC07 Plus Postage.
Document Type: CONFERENCE PROCEEDINGS (021)
Geographic Source: France
Government: International
This collection of eight essays examines the current and future status of early childhood education and care (educare), focusing on Europe but also addressing issues applicable to the wider world. The essays are: (1) "Early Childhood Intervention: An Overview of Practice North and South" (John Bennett); (2) "Developing the Child's Conception of Learning" (Ingrid Pramling); (3) Do Early Childhood Services Need a Coherent and Comprehensive Approach?" (Peter Moss); (4) "Children's Living Conditions, Secular Changes, and Childhood Mythology" (Dion Sommer); (5) "The Key to Quality is Qualifying the Teachers" (Mogens Nielsen); (6) "Appropriate Developmental Early Childhood Education" (David Weikart); (7) "The Experience of Reggio Emilia, a Place Where Adults and Children Learn Together" (Tiziana Filippini); and (8) "Epilogue" (Steen Larsen), a look at the importance of children's informal learning, which begins at birth. (MDM)
Descriptors: *Cognitive Development; Comprehensive Programs; *Early Childhood Education; *Educational Change; *Educational Quality; Family Environment; Foreign Countries; Learning Processes;

Student Centered Curriculum; Teacher Education; *Young Children
Identifiers: Developmentally Appropriate Programs; *Educare;
*Europe; Integrated Services; Italy (Reggio Emilia)

ED355034 PS021222
The Hundred Languages of Children:
The Reggio Emilia Approach to Early Childhood Education.
Edwards, Carolyn, Ed.; And Others
1993; 324p.
ISBN: 0-89391-933-0
Available From: Ablex Publishing Corporation, 355 Chestnut Street,
Norwood, NJ 07648 (hardcopy: ISBN-0-89391-927-6, $54.95;
paperback:
ISBN-0-89391-933-0, $24.95).
Document Not Available from EDRS.
Document Type: COLLECTION (020); PROJECT DESCRIPTION (141)
Geographic Source: U.S.; New Jersey
This collection of 18 essays and interviews documents the unique
approach to early childhood education taken by schools in the Reggio
Emilia region of Northern Italy for the last 30 years. The book is
divided into four major parts. Part I includes an introduction by Carolyn
Edwards and others, and the essay, "What Can We Learn From Reggio
Emilia?" by Lilian G. Katz, Part II consists of five interviews conducted
by Lella Gandini with Reggio Emilia educators: "History, Ideas, and
Basic Philosophy," with Loris Malaguzzi; "The Community-Teacher
Partnership in the Governance of the Schools," with Sergio Spaggiari;
"The Emergent Curriculum and Social Constructivism," with Carlina
Rinaldi; "The Role of the Pedagogista," with Tiziana Filippini; and
"The Role of the Atelierista," with Vea Vecchi. Part III examines the
theory and practice of the Reggio Emilia approach through four essays:
"Educational and Caring Spaces," by Lella Gandini; "Partner, Nurturer,
and Guide: The Roles of the Reggio Teacher in Action," by Carolyn
Edwards; "Multiple Symbolization in the Long Jump Project," by
George Forman; and "Curriculum Development in Reggio Emilia: A
Long-Term Curriculum Project About Dinosaurs," by Baji Rankin. Part
IV examines the extension of the Reggio Emilia approach to American
classrooms in six essays: "Cultural Variations on Developmentally
Appropriate Practice: Challenges to Theory and Practice," by Rebecca
New; "The City in the Snow: Applying the Multisymbolic Approach in
Massachusetts," by George Forman and others; "Connections: Using
the Project Approach with 2- and 3-Year-Olds in a University
Laboratory School," by Debbie LeeKeenan and John Nimmo; "Another
Way of Seeing Things: We're Still Learning," by Baji Rankin and
others; "A Backward Look: From Reggio Emilia to Progressive
Education," by Meg Barden; and "Poppies and the Dance of World
Making," by Paul Kaufman. A closing essay, "Conclusion: Where Do
We Go From Here?" by Carolyn Edwards and George Forman; a
glossary of terms used by Reggio Emilia educators; and a list of
published resources about the Reggio Emilia approach conclude the
volume. (MDM)
Descriptors: *Art Education; Community Role; Creative Development;

*Curriculum Development; Educational Innovation; *Educational
Methods; *Educational Theories; Foreign Countries; Preschool
Education; Progressive Education; Student Projects; Teacher Role;
*Young Children
Identifiers: *Italy (Reggio Emilia); *Massachusetts (Amherst); United States

ED354988 PS021008
Reggio Emilia: Some Lessons for U.S. Educators. ERIC Digest.
New, Rebecca S.
ERIC Clearinghouse on Elementary and Early Childhood Education,
Urbana, Ill.
1993; 3p.
Sponsoring Agency: Office of Educational Research and Improvement
(ED), Washington, DC.
Contract No: RI88062012
Report No: EDO-PS-93-3 EDRS Price - MF01/PC01 Plus Postage.
Document Type: ERIC PRODUCT (071)
Geographic Source: U.S.; Illinois
An internationally acclaimed program that challenges American
notions of appropriate early education is the municipal early childhood
program in Reggio Emilia, Italy. The town's liberal financial support of
child care and citizen membership in school committees indicate strong
community support. Parents are involved in school policy discussions,
child development concerns, and curriculum planning. The
administration of the early childhood program consists of a head
administrator, team leaders, and teachers. There is no hierarchical
relationship among teachers. Teacher in-service education is provided
through extensive staff development opportunities. The organization of
the physical environment of the school is crucial to the program. Spaces
are designed so that classrooms are integrated with the school and
schools with the surrounding community. Class activities include
projects that teachers work on with small groups of children. Project
topics are chosen based on teacher observations of children's play, or
teachers' or parents' academic curiosity. As they proceed in their
investigation of a topic, children are encouraged to depict their
understanding through drawing, sculpture, dramatic play, and writing.
Several characteristics of the Reggio Emilia approach that challenge
American conceptions of developmentally appropriate practice include
teachers' beliefs in the importance of being confused as a contributor to
learning and the importance of children's ability to negotiate in peer
groups. (Contains nine references.) (BC)
Descriptors: *Class Activities; *Community Support; Educational
Environment; Foreign Countries; Inservice Teacher Education; Parent
Participation; *Physical Environment; *Preschool Education;
*Program Administration; Program Descriptions; *Symbolic
Language; Teacher Student Relationship
Identifiers: ERIC Digests; *Italy (Reggio Emilia)

ED351123 PS020845
Making Meaning with Eyes and Hands.
Veale, Ann

Jun 1992; 12p.
EDRS Price - MF01/PC01 Plus Postage.
Document Type: PROJECT DESCRIPTION (141)
Geographic Source: Australia; South Australia
In light of criticisms that many early childhood programs fail to engage children's minds, this study suggests that children need programs in which they can: (1) explore experience in visual ways; (2) experience aspects of different cultures; (3) extend their thinking; and (4) develop their imagination. That art and play can provide suitable vehicles for these endeavors is suggested by curriculum theorist and art educator Elliot W. Eisner, and exemplified by the Reggio Emilia preschool art program in Italy, which encourages and records the long-term creative activities of children for the children's own later review. Exposure to family memorabilia, for example, can help stimulate children's visual experiences and heighten their sense of perception. Australian children also need to become aware of the various cultures of Southeast Asia and the art that those cultures have produced, so that the children can experience aspects of the cultures of nearby peoples. Early childhood art programs need to encourage children to become involved and absorbed in mind-engaging work for extended periods of time, so that they can edit and perfect their work and transform original ideas into imaginative variations. (MDM)
Descriptors: *Art Education; *Childrens Art; *Curriculum Development; Educational Theories; Foreign Countries; Imagination; Play; Preschool Education; *Visual Arts; *Young Children
Identifiers: Australia; *Eisner (Elliot W); *Italy (Reggio Emilia)

ED338386 PS019963
Impressions of Reggio Emilia.
Borgia, Eileen
15 Aug 1991; 35p.
EDRS Price - MF01/PC02 Plus Postage.
Document Type: PROJECT DESCRIPTION (141)
Geographic Source: Illinois
The preschools operated by the municipality of Reggio Emilia in Emilia Romagna, Italy, have drawn the attention of early childhood educators worldwide. This paper describes five features of these preschools. First, the educational philosophy of the schools is influenced by the high value accorded to cooperation in northern Italian culture; Bruner's concept of learning as a communal activity; and Issacs' concept of learning as active inquiry. Second, teachers are viewed as collaborators in a child's education, rather than as transmitters of knowledge, and there is frequent cooperation between teachers and parents concerning children's education. Third, the design of the preschools has incorporated aesthetically beautiful spaces, including spacious entryways, clean and decorated dining rooms, and well-supplied art areas. Fourth, great value is placed on arts and letters. Children's visual perception and aesthetic awareness are enhanced. Drawing is a daily occurrence. Teachers encourage children's communication through words and nonverbal means. Fifth, the preschools use the project approach to learning. Projects incorporate art, science, numbers, and words, and involve

discussions, field experience, cultural exposure, and relating to the community at large. A list of 20 references is included. (BC)

Descriptors: Aesthetic Education; Aesthetic Values; *Art Education; Communication Skills; *Cooperative Learning; *Educational Facilities Design; *Educational Philosophy; Experiential Learning; Foreign Countries; Parent Participation; Parent Teacher Cooperation; Preschool Children; *Preschool Education; Preschool Teachers; Student Projects; Teaching Methods

Identifiers: *Italy (Reggio Emilia)

ED319483 PS018748

Early Child Care and Education, Italian Style:
The Reggio Emilia Daycare and Preschool Program.
New, Rebecca S.
Nov 1989; 19p.
EDRS Price - MF01/PC01 Plus Postage.
Document Type: PROJECT DESCRIPTION (141)
Geographic Source: U.S.; New York

The municipal early childhood program in Reggio Emilia, Italy, one of the most renowned examples of community-supported child care systems in the Western world, is described. A brief historical overview is followed by discussion of such aspects of the Reggio Emilia project as the high level of exchange between families and schools, the predominance of aesthetic considerations throughout the schools, and the importance of the physical environment and use of classroom space in meeting curriculum goals. It is concluded that even though many features of the Reggio Emilia program reflect Italian cultural values and may be inappropriate for child care settings outside Italy, some aspects of the program are worth emulating. These include: (1) the emphasis on the positive value of multiple points of view and reciprocal participation in the family-school relationship; (2) the view that the dialogue between parents and teachers is and should be a complicated matter; (3) the emphases on the arts and aesthetic sensibilities; and (4) the significance of the environment as a provider of opportunities for social exchanges. (RH)

Descriptors: *Aesthetic Values; Boards of Education; Childrens Art; Community Programs; *Day Care; Early Childhood Education; *Educational Environment; Educational Facilities; Family School Relationship; Foreign Countries; *Parent Participation; *Preschool Curriculum; *Preschool Education; Program Descriptions; Public Schools; Record Keeping; School Organization; Space

Identifiers: *Italy (Reggio Emilia)

ED318565 PS018749

Projects and Provocations:
Preschool Curriculum Ideas from Reggio Emilia, Italy.
New, Rebecca S.
1990; 19p.
EDRS Price - MF01/PC01 Plus Postage.
Document Type: PROJECT DESCRIPTION (141)
Geographic Source: U.S.; New York

This paper explores implications of the preschool program in Reggio

Emilia, Italy for the early childhood education curriculum in the United States. Reggio Emilia's municipal early childhood program incorporates high quality day care with a carefully articulated philosophy of education. The curriculum of the preschools is based on a project approach to learning that emphasizes symbolic representation. Children and teachers are viewed as partners in learning. Teachers serve as facilitators of a constructivist curriculum: as provocateurs who create discontinuous or discrepant experiences and problems. Teachers also serve as careful observers who document children's growth. Teachers view art as central to the educational process, as a form of exploration and expression. Each preschool has an art teacher who is available to work with the children and their teachers throughout the day. Projects, which provide numerous opportunities for symbolic representation, may last for several days or months. A sequence of responding, recording, playing, exploring, hypothesis building and testing, and provoking occurs in most projects. The projects described in detail concern shadows, self-portraits, war play, enemies, and outer space. (RH)

Descriptors: Art Products; Communication (Thought Transfer); Curriculum Development; Early Childhood Education; *Educational Innovation; Foreign Countries; *Preschool Curriculum; Program Descriptions; Public Schools; *Student Projects; Student Role; *Teacher Role; Teacher Student Relationship; *Teaching Methods

Identifiers: *Italy; *Symbolic Representation

Journal Articles

EJ483344 EA529362
Lessons from Reggio Emilia.
Palestis, Ernest
Principal, v73 n5 p16-17,19 May 1994
ISSN: 0271-6062
Available From: UMI
Document Type: PROJECT DESCRIPTION (141); JOURNAL
ARTICLE (080)
Reggio Emilia's pioneering effort in preschool education has been
widely replicated throughout Italy, where almost 90% of nation's
children aged 3-6 enroll in national, municipal, private preschools.
These preschools are unlike any in the United States. There are no
building principals or school boards. America must invest more time,
money, and parent energy in preschool education. (MLH)
Descriptors: *Class Organization; *Comparative Education;
Cooperative Learning; Foreign Countries; Interdisciplinary Approach;
*Models; Parent Participation; Portfolios (Background Materials);
Preschool Education; *School Organization
Identifiers: *Italy; *Reggio Emilia Preschools

EJ481988 PS521558
Special Places for Children—The Schools in Reggio Emilia, Italy.
Gandini, Lella; And Others
Child Care Information Exchange, n96 p47-70 Mar-Apr 1994
ISSN: 0164-8527
Available From: UMI
Document Type: PROJECT DESCRIPTION (141); JOURNAL
ARTICLE (080)
Four articles discuss the child-centered approach of the preschools of
Reggio Emilia, Italy: "Not Just Anywhere: Making Child Care Centers
into 'Particular' Places" (Lella Gandini); "Your Image of the Child"
(Loris Malaguzzi); "What Can We Learn from Reggio Emilia: An
Italian-American Collaboration (Lella Gandini); and "Unpacking My
Questions and Images: Personal Reflections on Reggio Emilia"
(Bonnie Neugebauer). (MDM)
Descriptors: Art Education; Classroom Environment; *Educational
Improvement; Foreign Countries; Interviews; *Preschool Curriculum;
*Preschool Education; School Community Relationship; *Student
Centered Curriculum; *Teacher Attitudes
Identifiers: *Italy (Reggio Emilia)

EJ474815 PS521294
**Fundamentals of the Reggio Emilia Approach
to Early Childhood Education.**
Gandini, Lella
Young Children, v49 n1 p4-8 Nov 1993
ISSN: 0044-0728
Available From: UMI
Document Type: PROJECT DESCRIPTION (141); JOURNAL

ARTICLE (080)
Describes the experimental preschools of Reggio Emilia, Italy, providing a brief history and an overview of their guiding educational philosophy. Notes their distinguishing features, including an image of the child's social construction of learning, cognizance of children's sense of time, involvement of parents and the community, collaboration among teachers, a studio atmosphere, group projects, and extensive documentation. (ME)
Descriptors: Art Education; Classroom Design; *Cooperative Learning; *Experimental Schools; *Parent Participation; Preschool Education; *School Community Relationship; Student Projects; Teacher Role; *Teacher Student Relationship; *Teaching Methods; Time Factors (Learning)
Identifiers: *Italy (Reggio Emilia)

EJ474757 PS521104
Special Book Review Feature. The Hundred Languages of Children.
Phillips, Carol Brunson
Young Children, v49 n1 p17-18 Nov 1993
ISSN: 0044-0728
Available From: UMI
Document Type: BOOK-PRODUCT REVIEW (072); JOURNAL ARTICLE (080)
Reviews a volume edited by Carolyn Edwards, Lella Gandini, and George Forman, that presents a thorough overview of the educational philosophy and practices of the city-run early childhood program of Reggio Emilia, Italy. (ME)
Descriptors: Classroom Design; *Educational Philosophy; Parent Participation; Preschool Education; *School Community Relationship; Teacher Role; Teacher Student Relationship; *Teaching Methods
Identifiers: *Italy (Reggio Emilia)

EJ474756 PS521103
Reflections on Reggio Emilia.
Bredekamp, Sue
Young Children, v49 n1 p13-17 Nov 1993
ISSN: 0044-0728
Available From: UMI
Document Type: POSITION PAPER (120); JOURNAL ARTICLE (080)
Inspired by the early childhood schools of Reggio Emilia, Italy, offers six challenges to American educators to reclaim the image of the competent child, promote conceptual integrity of programs for children, refine the definition of developmental appropriateness, balance standard-setting with questioning, reflect on professional development, and expand teacher roles. (ME)
Descriptors: Childrens Rights; *Competence; *Educational Attitudes; *Educational Improvement; Educational Philosophy; Preschool Education; *Professional Development; *Standards; *Teacher Role
Identifiers: Italy (Reggio Emilia)

EJ474755 PS521102
For an Education Based on Relationships.
Malaguzzi, Loris
Young Children, v49 n1 p9-12 Nov 1993
ISSN: 0044-0728
Available From: UMI
Document Type: TRANSLATION (170); PROJECT DESCRIPTION (141); JOURNAL ARTICLE (080)
Outlines the educational philosophy of Loris Malaguzzi, founder of the experimental preschools of Reggio Emilia, Italy, which focuses on providing a physical and social environment for learning through interactions among children, teachers, and parents. Discusses formation of communications networks and 12 principles for organizing small group work, including colearning, age similarity, symbolic play, and cognitive conflicts. (ME)
Descriptors: Classroom Environment; Cognitive Dissonance; *Cooperative Learning; *Educational Philosophy; *Group Dynamics; Peer Relationship; Preschool Education; Pretend Play; Social Cognition; *Teacher Student Relationship
Identifiers: Child Behavior; *Italy (Reggio Emilia)

EJ473230 PS521057
Reviews of Professional Literature.
Williams, Peter A.; And Others
Dimensions of Early Childhood, v22 n1 p26-32 Fall 1993
ISSN: 0160-6425
Document Type: BOOK-PRODUCT REVIEW (072); JOURNAL ARTICLE (080)
Reviews the professional literature on such topics/issues in early childhood education as the Reggio Emilia approach; activity-based classrooms; use of learning centers in classrooms; storytelling, story dramatization and writing; story "stretchers" for primary grades; connections between body size and self-esteem; and early childhood intervention. (BB)
Descriptors: Body Weight; Book Reviews; *Day Care; Dramatics; Early Childhood Education; Early Intervention; *Expressive Language; Foreign Countries; *Learning Centers (Classroom); Self Esteem; Story Telling; *Teacher Role; *Young Children
Identifiers: *Activity Based Curriculum; *Italy (Reggio Emilia); Story Writing

EJ473227 PS521054
**Similarities between Early Childhood Education
in Oxfordshire, England and Reggio Emilia, Italy.**
Firlik, Russell J.
Dimensions of Early Childhood, v22 n1 p13,38-39 Fall 1993
ISSN: 0160-6425
Document Type: POSITION PAPER (120); JOURNAL ARTICLE (080)
Discusses four similarities between early childhood education systems in Oxfordshire, England and Reggio Emilia, Italy. Similarities between

the two school systems include an integrated curriculum; (mixed) age grouping and school organization; the teacher's role; and the pedagogical underpinnings. (BB)

Descriptors: British Infant Schools; Classroom Environment; Comparative Education; Early Childhood Education; Foreign Countries; *Foundations of Education; *Integrated Curriculum; *Multigraded Classes; Preschool Education; School Organization; *Teacher Role; *Teaching Methods; Young Children

Identifiers: England (Oxfordshire); *Italy (Reggio Emilia); Multi Age Grouping; Primary Schools (United Kingdom)

EJ473226 PS521053
Inviting Children into Project Work.
Edwards, Carolyn P.; Springate, Kay
Dimensions of Early Childhood, v22 n1 p9-12,40 Fall 1993
ISSN: 0160-6425
Document Type: PROJECT DESCRIPTION (141); TEACHING GUIDE (052); JOURNAL ARTICLE (080)
Illustrates how the Reggio Emilia (Italy) Approach to learning uses classroom projects to provide valuable learning experiences to young children. Suggests how certain aspects of the Reggio Emilia approach of classroom project work may be applied to teaching and learning strategies in the United States. (BB)

Descriptors: *Class Activities; Classroom Environment; *Day Care; Documentation; Early Childhood Education; Expressive Language; Foreign Countries; Integrated Activities; International Education; Program Descriptions; School Space; *Student Projects; Teacher Role; *Teaching Methods; *Young Children

Identifiers: *Italy (Reggio Emilia); *Learning Environment; Time Allocation

EJ471302 PS520641
A Disposition to Be Resourceful: An Interview with Lilian Katz.
Montessori Life, v5 n2 p26-30 Spr 1993
Document Type: POSITION PAPER (120); JOURNAL ARTICLE (080)
Lilian Katz is director of the ERIC Clearinghouse on Elementary and Early Childhood Education, professor at University of Illinois, and, in 1992, was elected president of National Association for Education of Young Children (NAEYC). Discussed are her background, early childhood teacher preparation, students' and teachers' dispositions, Montessori education, the Reggio Emilia preschool system, professionalization of teaching, and plans for NAEYC. (SM)

Descriptors: Childhood Attitudes; Day Care; *Early Childhood Education; Montessori Method; Personality Traits; *Preschool Teachers; Professional Recognition; Teacher Attitudes; Teacher Background; *Teacher Education; *Teacher Educators

Identifiers: Italy (Reggio Emilia); *Katz (Lilian G); National Association Educ of Young Children; Professionalization of Teaching

EJ446306 PS519496
Inviting Children's Creativity: A Story of Reggio Emilia, Italy.
Rankin, Baji
Child Care Information Exchange, n85 p30-35 May-Jun 1992
ISSN: 0164-8527
Available From: UMI
Language: English
Document Type: JOURNAL ARTICLE (080); PROJECT DESCRIPTION (141)
Target Audience: Teachers; Practitioners
Describes a student project of the Anna Frank school for three to six year olds in Reggio Emilia, Italy, in which students developed creativity by exploring the world of dinosaurs. Underscores the reciprocity between children and teachers in guiding the project. (AC)
Descriptors: *Classroom Environment; *Creative Development; Early Childhood Education; Educational Objectives; Foreign Countries; *Preschool Teachers; Program Descriptions; Science Instruction; *Student Projects; *Teacher Role; *Teacher Student Relationship; Young Children
Identifiers: Dinosaurs; *Italy (Reggio Emilia)

EJ446305 PS519495
Creativity Comes Dressed in Everyday Clothes.
Gandini, Lella
Child Care Information Exchange, n85 p26-29 May-Jun 1992
ISSN: 0164-8527
Available From: UMI
Document Type: JOURNAL ARTICLE (080); PROJECT DESCRIPTION (141)
Target Audience: Teachers; Administrators; Practitioners
Describes the early childhood system in Reggio Emilia, Italy, in which educators (1) ensure that children live in "a community of well-being"; (2) create a supportive environment; (3) respect individual rhythms; (4) maintain work areas for the visual arts; (5) respond flexibly to children; and (6) foster peer support. (AC)
Descriptors: *Classroom Environment; *Creative Development; *Creativity; Early Childhood Education; Educational Objectives; Foreign Countries; *Preschool Teachers; Program Descriptions; *Teacher Role; *Teacher Student Relationship; Young Children
Identifiers: *Italy (Reggio Emilia)

EJ446304 PS519494
Creativity and Learning.
Gandini, Lella; And Others
Child Care Information Exchange, n85 p25-40 May-Jun 1992
For individual articles in this pull-out section, see PS 519 495-498.
ISSN: 0164-8527
Available From: UMI
Document Type: JOURNAL ARTICLE (080); PROJECT DESCRIPTION (141); NON-CLASSROOM MATERIAL (055)

In this special section on creativity and learning, several articles discuss practices of schools in Reggio Emilia, Italy. Topics include the role of reciprocity between child and adult in creative learning; the importance of play for adults; and ideas directors can use to help teachers translate creativity into classroom practice. (AC)
Descriptors: *Classroom Environment; *Creative Development; *Creativity; Early Childhood Education; Educational Objectives; Foreign Countries; *Preschool Teachers; Program Descriptions; *Teacher Role; *Teacher Student Relationship; Young Children
Identifiers: *Italy (Reggio Emilia)

EJ415420 PS517977
Impressions of Reggio Emilia Preschools.
Katz, Lilian G.
Young Children, v45 n6 p11-12 Sep 1990
Report No: ISSN-0044-0728
Available From: UMI
Document Type: JOURNAL ARTICLE (080); POSITION PAPER (120)
The preschool program of Reggio Emilia, Italy is discussed in terms of the quality of the program's environment, the quality of its students' work, and student and teacher planning involved in the projects undertaken by the students. It is maintained that children in the Reggio Emilia program know what is important to the adults around them.(BG)
Descriptors: Childrens Art; *Educational Environment; *Preschool Children; *Preschool Curriculum; *Preschool Education; *Student Projects
Identifiers: *Italy (Reggio Emilia)

EJ415419 PS517976
Excellent Early Education: A City in Italy Has It.
New, Rebecca
Young Children, v45 n6 p4-10 Sep 1990
Report No: ISSN-0044-0728
Available From: UMI
Document Type: JOURNAL ARTICLE (080); PROJECT DESCRIPTION (141)
The preschool program of Reggio Emilia, Italy is discussed in terms of its commitment to the community, its project- and art- based curriculum, its use of space to support curriculum goals, and characteristics of its environment. Implications of the program for American education are discussed. (BG)
Descriptors: Aesthetic Education; Art Activities; *Educational Environment; Grouping (Instructional Purposes); Parent Participation; *Preschool Children; *Preschool Curriculum; *Preschool Education; *School Community Relationship; Space Utilization; Student Projects
Identifiers: Italy (Reggio Emilia)

Additional Resources on Reggio Emilia and the Reggio Emilia Approach

Books

CORSARO, W.A., and F. EMILIANI. (1992). Child care, early education and children's peer culture in Italy. In M.E. Lamb, K.J. Sternberg, C.P. Hwang, and A.G. Bromberg (Eds.), Child care in context: Cross-cultural perspectives (pp. 81-115). Hillsdale, NJ: Lawrence Erlbaum.

DEPARTMENT OF EARLY EDUCATION, City of Reggio Emilia. (1987). I centro linguaggi dei bambini. (The hundred languages of children: Narrative of the possible). Catalog of the exhibit, "The hundred languages of children," in Italian and English. Reggio Emilia, Italy: Author. (Assessorato Scuole Infanzia e Asili Nido, Via Guido da Castello 12, 42100 Reggio Emilia, Italy).

DEPARTMENT OF EARLY EDUCATION, City of Reggio Emilia. (1990). An historical outline, data and information. Reggio Emilia, Italy: Author.

EDWARDS, C.P., G. FORMAN, and L. GANDINI. (Eds.). (In press). Education for all the children: The multi-symbolic approach to early education in Reggio Emilia, Italy. Norwood, NJ: Ablex.

FORMAN, G. (1989). Helping children ask good questions. In Bonnie Neugebauer (Ed.), The wonder of exploring how the world works (pp. 21-24). Redmond, WA: Exchange Press.

FORMAN, G. (1992). The constructivist perspective. In J.L. Roopnarine, and J.E. Johnson (Eds.), Approaches to early childhood education. Columbus, OH: Merrill.

GANDINI, L. (1988). Children and parents at bedtime: Physical closeness during the rituals of separation. Unpublished doctoral dissertation, School of Education, University of Massachusetts, Amherst.

MILLSOM, C. (1994). An inspiring example of community-supported day care: Reggio Emilia, Italy. In H. Nuba, M. Searson, and D.L. Sheiman (Eds.), Resources for early childhood. New York: Garland Publishing.

PISTILLO, F. (1989). Preprimary education and care in Italy. In P. Olmsted, and D. Weikart (Eds.), How nations serve young children: Profiles of child care and education in 14 countries (pp. 151-202). Ypsilanti, MI: High Scope.

RABITTI, G. (1994). Alla scoperta della dimensione perduta: L'etnografia dell'educazione in una scuola dell'infanzia di Reggio Emilia. Bologna, Italy: Cooperativa Libraria Universitaria Editrice Bologna.

WHITING, B.B., and C.P. EDWARDS. (1988). Children of different worlds: The formation of social behavior. Cambridge, MA: Harvard University Press.

Journal Articles

CLARK, K. (1994). How do caterpillars make cocoons? A Kentucky kindergarten investigates in an adaptation of the Reggio Emilia approach. Dimensions of Early Education 22(3, Spring):5-9.

DOLCI, M. (1994). When the wolf both is and is not a wolf: The language of puppets. Child Care Information Exchange (98, July/August):43-46.

EDWARDS, C.P., L. GANDINI, and J. NIMMO. (1992). Favorire l'apprendimento cooperativo nella prima infanzia. (Promoting collaborative learning in the early childhood classroom). Rassegna di Psicologia, no. 3. University of Rome.

EDWARDS, C.P., D.J. SHALLCROSS, and J. MALONEY. (1991). Promoting creativity in a graduate course on creativity: Entering the time and space of the young child. Journal of Creative Behavior 25(4):304-310.

GANDINI, L. (1992). Creativity comes dressed in everyday clothes. Child Care Information Exchange (85, Summer):85-89.

GANDINI, L. (1994). Not just anywhere: Making child care centers into "particular" places. Child Care Information Exchange (96, March/April):48-51.

GANDINI, L. (1994). What can we learn from Reggio Emilia: An Italian-American collaboration. An interview with Amelia Gambetti and Mary Beth Radke. Child Care Information Exchange (96, March/April):62-66.

GANDINI, L., and C. EDWARDS. (1988). Early childhood integration of the visual arts. Gifted International 5(2):14-18.

LEEKEENAN, D., and C. EDWARDS. (1992). Using the project approach with toddlers. Young Children 47(May, 4):31-35.

LEWIN, A.W. (1992). The view from Reggio. Hand to Hand: Youth Museums Newsletter 6(1):4-6.

MALAGUZZI, LORIS. (1994). Your image of the child: Where teaching begins. Child Care Information Exchange (96, March/April):52-61.

NEUGEBAUER, B. (1994). Unpacking my questions and images: Personal reflections on Reggio Emilia. Child Care Information Exchange (96, March/April):67-70.

NEW, R. (1991). Early childhood teacher education in Italy: Reggio Emilia's master plan for "master" teachers. The Journal of Early Childhood Teacher Education 12(37):3.

TREPANIER-STREET, M. (1993). What's so new about the project approach? Childhood Education 70(1, Fall):25-28.
Tribute to Loris Malaguzzi. (1994). Young Children 49(5, July):55.

Videotapes

Childhood. (1991). By PBS. Short segments on Reggio Emilia in Parts 3 and 4. Ambrose Video Publishing, 1290 Avenue of the Americas, Suite 2245, New York, NY 10104.

The creative spirit. (1992). By PBS. Segment on Reggio Emilia in Part 2. PBS Video, 4401 Sunset Boulevard, Los Angeles, CA 90027. Companion volume: Goleman, D., P. Kaufman, and M. Ray. (1992). The creative spirit. New York: Dutton.

Early learning in Reggio Emilia, Italy. (1993). A clear overview of the total programs in Reggio Emilia presented with slides by Dr. Brenda Fyfe. Distributed by Project Apples, 27 Horrabin Hall, College of Education, Western Illinois University, Macomb, IL 61455; (309) 298-1634.

The long jump: A video analysis of small group projects in early education as practiced in Reggio Emilia, Italy. (1991). By George Forman and Lella Gandini. Performanetics Press, 19 The Hollow, Amherst, MA 01002; (413) 256-8846.

To make a portrait of a lion. (1987). Comune di Reggio Emilia, Centro Documentazione Ricerca Educativa Nidi e Scuole dell'Infanzia. Available through: Baji Rankin, 346 Washington St., Cambridge, MA 02139.

A message from Malaguzzi. (1993). A one-hour video of an interview with Loris Malaguzzi. Produced by George Forman and Lella Gandini. Available through: Performanetics Press, 19 The Hollow, Amherst, MA 01002; (413) 256-8846.

Additional Resources

Educational Foundations

Reggio Children S.r.l.
Via Guido da Castello, 12
42100 Reggio Emilia, Italy

This foundation seeks to increase awareness of the Reggio Emilia approach to the education of young children.

Reggio Children/U.S.A.
1341 G Street, N.W., Suite 400
Washington, DC 20005
phone: (202) 265-9090

Newsletters

U.S.-Reggio Emilia Network Newsletter. Published by the Merrill-Palmer Institute, 71A East Ferry Avenue, Detroit, MI 48202.

Innovations in Early Education: The International Reggio Exchange. This newsletter is published four times a year by the Merrill-Palmer Institute. Those interested in Reggio Emilia and the Reggio Emilia approach can read about the educational philosophy and strategies of the Italian programs and their adaptations elsewhere; keep up with conferences and workshops related to the Reggio Emilia approach; read about the experiences and impressions of Reggio Emilia educators and of American visitors to Reggio Emilia; engage in an international dialogue focused on enhancing the lives of children through educational-social systems; and experience some of the excitement that many teachers have found through exploring the Reggio Emilia approach.

Subscriptions to Innovations are $20 per year ($25 per year for foreign subscriptions). To subscribe, send a check to, or for more information contact:
The Merrill-Palmer Institute
Wayne State University
71-A E. Ferry Ave.
Detroit, MI 48202

REGGIO-L Listserv

A listserv is an electronic discussion group on the Internet. REGGIO-L is a listserv dedicated to Reggio Emilia and the Reggio Emilia approach. On REGGIO-L, early childhood educators, researchers, students, parents, and others who have an ongoing interest in the Reggio Emilia approach to early childhood education can discuss the educational philosophy behind the Reggio Emilia program, teaching approaches and essential elements of the program, its adaptation in the United States, and other related topics. The listserv is available 24 hours a day, 7 days a week!

REGGIO-L is co-owned by the Merrill-Palmer Institute at Wayne State University and the ERIC Clearinghouse on Elementary and Early Childhood Education (ERIC/EECE) at the University of Illinois.
Note that there are two email addresses associated with the REGGIO-L listserv discussion group (as with all listserv discussion groups). The administrative listserv address for REGGIO-L is:

listserv@vmd.cso.uiuc.edu

To subscribe to REGGIO-L, send an email message to this address. Leave the subject line blank. In the body of the message, type only the following:

subscribe REGGIO-L YourFirstName YourLastName

For example, if you are Jane Doe and you wants to subscribe to REGGIO- L, you would type:

subscribe REGGIO-L Jane Doe

You will automatically be subscribed to REGGIO-L. You will receive back via email a notice of your subscription and information about the listserv and about how to unsubscribe from the listserv. Please print out and keep this information for future reference.

The second email address associated with REGGIO-L is the discussion list address. Use this address to post a message that you want all members of the discussion group to see. Do not post messages intended for the listserv administration to the list address. The discussion list address for REGGIO-L is:

REGGIO-L@vmd.cso.uiuc.edu

The co-owners of REGGIO-L are:

Amy Aidman   Patricia Weissman
ERIC/EECE   Merrill-Palmer Institute
a-aidman@uiuc.edu   usergmrm@mts.cc.wayne.edu

If you have any questions about subscribing to REGGIO-L, contact:

Amy Aidman
ERIC/EECE
Phone: 800/583-4135; 217/333-1386
Email: a-aidman@uiuc.edu

How to Obtain Copies of ERIC Documents and Journal Articles

Most ERIC documents (EDs) are available from the ERIC Document Reproduction Service (EDRS). EDRS can be contacted at:

ERIC Document Reproduction Service
CBIS Federal, Inc.
7420 Fullerton Road, Suite 110
Springfield, Virginia, 22153-2852.
Telephone: 1-800-443-ERIC or 1-703-440-1400
Fax orders: 1-703-440-1408

Most documents in the preceding bibliography are available in microfiche (MF) and paper copy (PC). Publications that are not available from EDRS are listed with an alternate source and ordering information; citations to many publications that are available from ERIC also include an alternate source of availability.
ERIC journal articles (EJs) are available in the original journal, in libraries, through interlibrary loan, or from the following organizations:

UMI Article Clearinghouse
300 N. Zeeb Road
Ann Arbor, MI 48106
Telephone: 1-800-521-0600, ext. 2533 or 2534
Fax: 1-313-665-7075

Institute for Scientific Information(ISI)
Genuine Article Service
3501 Market Street
Philadelphia, PA 19104
Telephone: 1-800-523-1850

For a free list of ERIC microfiche collections in the United States and other countries, call or write to ACCESS ERIC at 1- 800-LET-ERIC.

The ERIC System

The Educational Resources Information Center (ERIC) is a national education information network designed to provide education information users with ready access to an extensive body of education-related literature. Established in 1966, ERIC is supported by the U.S. Department of Education, Office of Educational Research and

Improvement (OERI). The ERIC database is created by the 16 clearinghouses in the ERIC system. This database is the world's largest source of education information, containing more than 800,000 summaries of documents and journal articles on education research and practice. ERIC offers a document delivery service for the documents it collects and summarizes, many of which are unpublished.

The ERIC database can be used by consulting the print indexes Resources in Education (RIE) and Current Index to Journals in Education (CIJE) at more than 2,800 libraries and other locations worldwide; by using online search services (usually for a fee); by accessing ERIC at several sites on the Internet; by searching ERIC on CD-ROM at many libraries and information centers; or on the local computer systems of a growing number of universities and colleges. The database is updated monthly online and quarterly on CD-ROM. For more information on how to access the ERIC database, call ACCESS ERIC at its toll free number, 1-800-LET-ERIC. ACCESS ERIC informs callers of the services and products offered by ERIC components and other education information service providers.

The ERIC System, through its 16 subject-specific clearinghouses and four support components, provides a variety of services and products that can help individuals interested in education stay up to date on a broad range of education-related issues. Products include research summaries, publications on topics of high interest, newsletters, and bibliographies. ERIC system services include computer search services, reference and referral services, and document reproduction. Additional information on the ERIC system, including a list of ERIC clearinghouses and the subject areas they cover, is also available from ACCESS ERIC.

The ERIC Clearinghouse on Elementary and Early Childhood Education (ERIC/EECE)

The ERIC Clearinghouse on Elementary and Early Childhood Education (ERIC/EECE) has been located at the University of Illinois at Urbana-Champaign since 1967. The clearinghouse identifies, selects, and processes the report literature, books, and journal articles on topics related to the development, care, and education of children through early adolescence (except for specific subject areas covered by other ERIC clearinghouses) for the ERIC database.

The clearinghouse also provides other products and services, many of them at no cost. Free products include a biannual newsletter; ERIC Digests and resource lists on topics of high interest to parents, educators, policymakers, and the general public; brochures and publications lists; and ERIC system materials. Major publications, ReadySearches, and a subscription newsletter on mixed-age grouping in preschool and elementary school programs are available at low cost. In response to queries from the general public, the clearinghouse provides free materials, short searches of the ERIC database, and referrals to other information sources when appropriate. Other clearinghouse services include conducting workshops and making presentations; providing camera-ready materials for conferences; and conducting extensive computer searches (for a fee) on topics related to the clearinghouse scope of interest.

Please write or call the clearinghouse for additional information on any of these services or products, or to be placed on the clearinghouse mailing list.

ERIC/EECE
University of Illinois
805 W. Pennsylvania Avenue
Urbana, IL 61801-4897
Telephone: 217-333-1386
Fax: 217-333-3767
Email:ericeece@ux1.cso.uiuc.edu

Table of Contents